WATER INTO WINE?

An Investigation of the Concept of Miracle

The possible or actual occurrence of miracles has been vigorously debated. Robert Larmer here re-examines significant issues in this debate and attacks two basic assumptions governing it.

The first is that a miracle, understood as an event produced by a transcendent agent overriding the usual course of nature, involves a violation of the laws of nature. Larmer argues that events are explained by reference to both relevant laws and the units of mass / energy in the sequences to be explained. A miracle then need not be conceived as involving a violation of natural law, but rather as the creation or annihilation of units of mass / energy by a transcendent agent. In reply to the objection that this account would violate the first law of thermodynamics, he distinguishes two forms of the principle – one metaphysical, one scientific – and argues that a miracle would not violate the principle considered as a scientific law.

The second assumption is that miracle testimony cannot serve as evidence for theism. Larmer demonstrates that the logical ties connecting the concept of miracle to theism need not imply that one must be a theist to evaluate miracle testimony properly. One need only be prepared to entertain theism as a hypothesis.

Attacking these assumptions allows Larmer to show that Humean "balance-of-probabilities" arguments, based on a presumed conflict between evidence that establishes belief in the laws of nature and evidence in favour of miracles, miss the point if miracles are not defined as violations of the laws of nature. In the absence of a general argument demonstrating that the testimonial evidence in favour of miracles conflicts with the evidence for the laws of nature, the atheist must demonstrate, on a case-by-case basis, why the testimonial evidence is to be rejected. The burden of proof, the author concludes, is not on the theist, but on the atheist.

Robert Larmer is a member of the Department of Philosophy at the University of New Brunswick.

Water into Wine?

AN INVESTIGATION OF THE CONCEPT OF MIRACLE

Robert A.H. Larmer

McGill-Queen's University Press
Kingston and Montreal

This book has been published with the help of a grant
from the Canadian Federation for the Humanities, using
funds provided by the Social Sciences and Humanities
Research Council of Canada.

Printed on acid-free paper

Canadian Cataloguing in Publication Data

Larmer, Robert A., 1954–
Water into wine: an investigation of the
concept of miracle
Includes index.
Bibliography: p.
ISBN 0-7735-0615-2
1. Miracles.   I. Title.
BT97.2.L37 1988   231.7'3   C87-090252-0

In memory of my mother Gladys M. Larmer,
a woman of quiet love and generosity

Contents

Preface / ix

1 The Task of Definition / 3

2 Miracles and the Laws of Nature / 17

3 David Hume and Prior Probability / 31

4 Further Objections to Miracles / 43

5 Physicalism and the Conservation of Energy / 61

6 World-Views and Falsification / 75

7 Miracles and Evidence / 93

8 Miracles and Apologetics / 111

Notes / 131

Bibliography / 143

Index / 151

Preface

Colin Brown, in his excellent work *Miracles and the Critical Mind*, remarks that studies of miracles tend to be either philosophical or exegetical. The reason for this is not hard to fathom. In an age of increasing specialization it is no easy matter to follow a debate across disciplinary boundaries, yet speak with any degree of authority. In one sense, this book is no exception to the general rule. Lacking special training in fields other than philosophy, I have chosen to limit my discussion to the philosophical issues surrounding the concept of miracle. It is not my view, however, that philosophical debate should be independent of existential concerns, or that its results have no implications for those involved in other disciplines. My arguments are meant to bear on the practical matter of evaluating miracle-claims and are, in fact, a product of my coming to grips with the New Testament.

My aim, of course, has been to explore the concept of miracle in a systematic and comprehensive way. The topic of miracles is a popular one in contemporary philosophy of religion and I have learned much from the lively and ongoing debate taking place in the journals. I take issue, however, with two very general assumptions that dominate this debate.

The first is the assumption that because, by definition, miracles are violations of the laws of nature, any evidence for them must conflict with the vast amount of evidence supporting belief in the laws of nature. I think it is possible to retain the traditional view that miracles come about through God overriding nature, yet not define miracles as violations of the laws of nature. If I am right in this, there is no reason to think that the evidence supporting belief in miracles conflicts with the evidence which supports our scientific understanding of natural phenomena. This would imply that Humean "balance-of-probabilities" arguments, depending as they do upon a presumed conflict between these two bodies of evidence, miss the point entirely. A consequence of this is that the burden of proof will be upon the critic, not the theist. If there is no necessary conflict of evidence then it is up to the critic, on a case-by-case basis, to justify her rejection of *prima facie* evidence that miracles occur.

The second is the assumption that miracle-testimony can play no part in establishing the truth of theism, since to call an event a miracle is already to presuppose the existence of God. While I agree that the concept of miracle has logical ties to theism, I do not think these are of a kind that require accepting theism before one can be properly open to miracle-testimony. If I am right in this the "apologetic from history" so beloved by writers of the eighteenth century is a lot more philosophically respectable than most contemporary thinkers have been willing to allow.

This book, then, is an attempt to refute these assumptions and place the debate on a new footing.

I would like to express my gratitude to a number of people associated with this book. My wife, Lorena, my family, my friends, especially those connected with Community House in Ottawa, have all encouraged me and provided me with opportunities for growth. One of the few regrets associated with this book is that my mother, to whom it is dedicated, did not live to see it in print. Some of my fondest memories of her are associated with the writing of this book during my summers on our family farm. My debt both to her and my father is immense.

I would like to thank Professors William Dray, Benoit Garceau, Andrew Lugg, and John Thorp. I have learned much through their criticism and encouragement. Especial thanks are due to John Thorp, who supervised the MA thesis out of which this book grew, and to Andrew Lugg, who was generous enough to read and offer valuable criticism on an earlier version of this manuscript.

Thanks are also due to the editors of *Dialogue* and *Sophia* for granting permission to use material that appeared in an earlier form in two articles: "Miracles and the Laws of Nature," *Dialogue* 24 (1985): 227–35; and "Miracles and Criteria," *Sophia* 23, no. 1 (1984): 4–10.

WATER INTO WINE?

CHAPTER ONE

The Task of Definition

It is important to be clear on what we mean by a miracle. I shall begin, therefore, by defining the term. Only if we can be clear on what we think a miracle is does it become possible to discuss questions of whether they occur and in what circumstances. A problem we immediately face, however, is that the word *miracle*, like a good many other words, is used in a number of different ways. For my purposes, I shall distinguish between two major uses which I term *subjective* and *objective*. Before attempting any formal definition, I want to say a few words about each of these uses and indicate the one with which I am concerned.

TWO USES OF "MIRACLE"

I begin with the subjective use of the term. What we notice in examining this use is that the word *miracle* is used not to describe some objective feature of an event, but rather the reaction of a particular subject to it. Like the word *nice*, the word *miracle* is often used to describe an observer's reaction to the event, not the event itself. When used this way, we get not a description of an event, but a description of the effect of that event upon some observer. By way of example, consider the case of a not particularly religious student who, upon unexpectedly passing a difficult examination, exclaims "It's a miracle I passed." Probably the student does not mean to say "This is an event which would not have occurred had not God intervened." Probably she means to say something along the lines of, "Although it is likely that this event has a perfectly natural explanation, I find it unexpected and astonishing." She is commenting not so much upon the event itself, as the effect it has had upon her state of mind.

In contrast, we find that the objective use of the word *miracle* focuses much more upon the event itself. When it is used in this way, implicit in calling an event a miracle is the claim that it was supernaturally caused. As Antony Flew notes, although this sense of the word "includes the idea that wonder is called for as at least part of the appropriate response, the crux as well as the ground for the wonder is that a miracle should consist in an overriding of the order of nature."[1] Consider the case of a terminally ill patient who, after a period of prayer both by himself and his friends, is informed by the doctors that his supposedly fatal case of cancer has completely disappeared and exclaims "It's a miracle that I have been healed." Probably he does not mean to say, "I feel sure that this event has a perfectly natural explanation, but I find it unexpected and astonishing." Probably he means to say something considerably stronger, namely "This is an event which never would have occurred had God not interfered with the regular course of nature and I feel wonder and thankfulness that He would do this."

Two points deserve emphasis here. The first is that the crucial element of difference between these two uses of the word *miracle* is not that one implies a subjective response of wonder and astonishment while the other does not, but that one specifies certain ontological considerations which make wonder and astonishment an appropriate response, whereas the other does not. The second is that the objective use of the word *miracle* is of greater philosophical and methodological interest than is its subjective use. If we adopt the subjective use of the term and say that so long as someone finds an event wonderful and astonishing that person cannot be wrong in calling it a miracle, there is very little left to be said. However, if there are certain ontological considerations which make wonder and astonishment either appropriate or inappropriate then there is a great deal to be said. I propose, therefore, to work with the objective sense of the word *miracle*.

FOUR ELEMENTS OF THE MIRACULOUS

The immediate project, then, is to arrive at a definition which expresses the way *miracle* is used in its objective sense. Two errors must be avoided. First, it is crucial that our definition capture all the basic elements present in this idea of the miraculous. Otherwise a truncated definition incapable of doing justice to the concept it is supposed to define will result. Second, it is essential that our definition exclude extraneous elements not vital to the concept. If we fail in excluding these elements we almost certainly will arrive at a definition which has different implications than those drawn from a more correct definition. We must, therefore, proceed very cautiously. Our aim is not to say too little or too much, neither to ignore the essential nor to introduce the extraneous. With this in mind, I propose to discuss briefly the basic ideas associated with the concept of a miracle when that term is used in its objective sense. I will then be in a position to propose a definition.

There are four basic ideas associated with the objective sense of the word *miracle*. One of these has already been mentioned, namely the idea that a miracle is a physical event which is beyond the ability of an unaided nature to produce. Also central, however, are the ideas that a miracle is brought about by a rational agent; that it is an event of an extraordinary kind; and that it has religious significance.

The idea that a miracle is a physical event which is beyond the ability of nature to produce is essentially an expression of our conviction that a miracle is super-naturally caused. We are convinced that it cannot be explained in terms of the normal workings of nature, but demands explanation in terms of something, or better, someone, acting upon nature. It is an event which demands an explanation in terms of a transcendent cause.

Not all philosophers would agree that this idea is basic to the notion of the miraculous. R.F. Holland and a number of others have argued that we need not always regard a miracle as the result of an overriding of nature. Holland provides us with the following example of a "miracle."

A child riding his toy motor-car strays on to an unguarded railway crossing near his house and a wheel of his car gets stuck down the side of one of the rails. An express train is due to pass with the signals in its favor and a curve in the track makes it impossible for the driver to stop his train in time to avoid any obstruction he might encounter on the crossing. The mother coming out of the house to look for her child sees him on the crossing and hears the train approaching. She runs forward shouting and waving. The little boy remains seated in his car looking downward, engrossed in the task of pedaling it free. The brakes of the train are applied and it comes to rest a few feet from the child. The mother thanks God for the miracle; which she never ceases to think of as such although, as she in due course learns, there was nothing supernatural about the manner in which the brakes of the train came to be applied. The driver had fainted, for a reason that had nothing to do with the presence of the child on the line, and the brakes were applied automatically as his hand ceased to exert pressure on the control lever. He fainted on this particular afternoon because his blood pressure had risen after an exception-ally heavy lunch during which he had quarrelled with a colleague, and the change in blood pressure caused a clot of blood to be dis-lodged and circulate. He fainted at the time when he did on the afternoon in question because this was the time at which the coagulation in his blood stream reached the brain.[2]

On the basis of this example, Holland argues that a miracle need not be regarded as an overriding of nature, but merely as an unusual and religiously significant coincidence. He comments:

The significance of some coincidences as opposed to others arises from their relation to human needs and hopes and fears, their effects for good or ill upon our lives. So we speak of our luck (fortune, fate, etc.) And the kind of thing that, outside religion, we call luck is in religious parlance the grace of God or a miracle of God ... But although a coincidence can be taken religiously as a sign and called a miracle and made the subject of a vow, it cannot without confusion be taken as a sign of divine interference with the natural order.[3]

There is a problem with this view, however. Holland fails to recognize that the believer, in calling it a miracle, is not just describing the event and the emotional impact it had on her, but making an ontological claim about its origin and cause. He ignores the fact that those who accord religious significance to the "coincidence" by which the child's life was preserved do not really regard it as a coincidence, at least not in the sense in which that word is usually understood.[4] Generally, *coincidence* is used to refer to remarkable or noteworthy instances of fortuitous concurrence. Those who would want to call an event such as Holland describes a miracle would not see it as a fortuitous event, that is, one produced by chance and not design. Typically, they would feel that God was involved in producing the event, either directly or indirectly. They might argue that the explanatory background is not as complete as Holland claims and that the event never would have occurred had not God at some point directly intervened so as to alter the course of nature. Alternatively, they might argue that, even though the event was the result of converging independent causal chains with which God did not interfere, it was nevertheless prearranged by God – that is, it was part of God's preordained plan and that when He created the universe He designed it in such a way that it would give rise to the event at precisely the time it did. Either view, however, makes the event the result of God's purposeful action and not a mere coincidence which nature, so to speak, threw up on its own.[5] Holland is wrong, therefore, to link the notion of miracle with the notion of coincidence.

But what of this idea that God might have designed nature so as to produce certain extraordinary and religiously significant events? Does it not force us to revise the claim that a miracle is an event which nature would not produce on its own? I think not. Certainly at a phenomenological level believers attempt to distinguish between religiously significant events viewed as indirectly produced by God (events which they feel God designed nature to produce), and religiously significant events viewed as directly produced by God (events which would never have occurred had God not overridden the usual course of nature). They are apt to categorize the first class as providential events, the second as miracles. Without wanting to claim that this analysis exhausts the idea of providential events, I do want to claim that our standard use of the word *miracle* implies something stronger than the mere prearranged convergence of independent causal chains. This notion simply cannot do justice to paradigmatic cases such as the Resurrection or the multiplying of the loaves and fishes. In order to account for these cases we must introduce the idea that a miracle involves the active overriding of nature.

A miracle, then, is an event which nature would not produce on its own; it is supernaturally caused and involves an overriding of the usual course of nature. This brings us to a second idea associated with the miraculous, namely that a miracle is brought about by a rational agent who transcends nature. A miracle is the result of an agent not bound by nature, or at least not entirely bound by nature, acting upon nature to produce an event which would not have otherwise occurred.

Whether or not this agent must be God or whether some lesser created agent might conceivably work a miracle is not always agreed upon. Some philosophers and theologians have wanted to insist that only God can work miracles. Yet, *prima facie*, it seems conceivable that beings other than God might produce miracles. There seems no absurdity in supposing that an angel might cause a miracle and there are reports in which the alleged agent of the miracle is a person, as in Acts 3:1-9. To insist that only God can work a miracle is to place upon the term a restriction inconsistent with the way in which it is generally used. Far more plausible is the view that all that is required is an agent who, to some degree, transcends nature.

Another idea associated with the notion of the miraculous is that a miracle is an unusual event. It constitutes an exception to the normal pattern of events in the natural world. It need not be absolutely unique; the fact that Christ multiplied loaves and fishes on more than one occasion will scarcely persuade us that these events were not miracles. But it must be extraordinary in some sense. Must this extraordinary character be easily recognizable, however? Events such as Christ walking on water or feeding the five thousand are clearly unusual and exceptions to the normal course of nature. Yet some philosophers have argued that the fact that the event is unusual and extraordinary need not be apparent. They have tried to show that unperceived miracles – events which are miraculous but which we do not recognize as such – may conceivably occur. David Hume, for example, argues that:

A miracle may either be discovered by men or not. This alters not its nature and essence. The raising of a house or ship into the air is a visible miracle. The raising of a feather, when the wind wants ever so little of a force requisite for that purpose, is as real a miracle, though not so sensible with regard to us.[6]

How this question is resolved will depend largely upon how a miracle is defined. At present I wish merely to say that I think Hume is wrong on this point. My grounds for saying this will be clear when I come to define what a miracle is.

Finally, there is the idea that a miracle must be an event of religious significance. We refuse to accept the view that it might be the result of an arbitrary or capricious act. We insist that if an event is to be called a miracle then it must be possible to interpret it as contributing towards a holy and divine purpose. It is this connection with the idea of a divine purpose which explains the view of many writers that miracles are not events contrary to nature, but events which fulfil nature. As Richard Swinburne remarks,

while an event which is a miracle is not in accordance with the nature of the objects involved in it, it is nevertheless in accordance with the divinely ordained natural order as a whole ... Miracles are events with a point in the overall scheme of things and so in a sense very regular.[7]

An objection which is sometimes raised at this point is that

there appears to be no set of objective independent criteria by which the theist can determine in all cases whether an event contributes to some holy, just purpose. Rather, the theist may in some cases be able to declare that an event contributes to a holy purpose only after she has determined that it has been caused by God.[8]

The theist, then, seems to be arguing in a circle, since it is only on the basis of her belief that an unusual event was caused by God that she accords it religious significance. This objection seems misguided, however. First, it seems to assume that only God can perform miracles. This, as I have just argued, seems an unduly restrictive use of the term *miracle*. Second, and more important, it ignores the fact that it makes no sense to call an event a miracle unless it can be interpreted as being in accord with the divine purposes. When we call an event a miracle we are claiming not only that it is an exception to the usual course of nature, but that it was produced by a transcendent agent overriding nature in order to fulfil some divine purpose. It is simply wrong, therefore, to assume that we could ever identify an unusual event *as a miracle*, prior to our judgment that it has religious significance, that it can plausibly be interpreted as fulfilling the purposes of God. The theist, then, is not arguing in a circle when she appeals to the idea of religious significance.

Obviously, what is meant by religious significance varies. Some writers have insisted that it be understood in an extremely narrow sense. They have insisted that a miracle must occur in an explicitly religious context and be seen to confirm a specific doctrine. Others have argued for a broader understanding of "religious significance" and contend that all that is required is that a miracle be consistent with God's purposes. Without wanting to deny that a miracle may, on occasion, be performed in order to validate a certain doctrine or claim, I think it clear that the latter view is the correct one. The key issue is whether the event is consistent with God's purposes broadly understood, not with whether it guarantees a doctrinal truth. Psychologically, it may be easier for many people to "see" a particular event as fulfilling God's purposes and having religious significance if it is understood as confirming a particular doctrine, but to insist that unless it does this it could not be a miracle is to forget that God may have other purposes, such as healing the sick, comforting the discouraged, or reviving religious awareness. Traditionally conceived, God is concerned not just with the conveying of propositional truths, but also with the welfare of His creatures. It is theologically naive, therefore, to think that in general the sole or even chief purpose of a miracle is to guarantee the truth of the system in which it occurs.[9]

DEFINING A MIRACLE

Having examined the basic elements inherent in the objective sense of the miraculous, the problem which faces us is to articulate a definition which does justice to these elements. Although these four ideas are basic, they may be treated in slightly different ways. So treated, they yield two related, but different, definitions. I shall briefly describe these two ways of defining a miracle and say which one is the more adequate.

One way of treating these four ideas is to treat the first two as together comprising a definition and the second two as yielding criteria by which a miracle is recognized. On this interpretation a miracle is a physical event which never would have occurred except through the action of a rational agent who transcends nature. Such an event is recognized and termed miraculous if it is of an extraordinary kind and is seen to have religious significance. This understanding of the term allows that there may occur unperceived miracles, but insists that we can only recognize as miraculous an event which is extraordinary and religiously significant.

Another way is to treat all four ideas as together comprising a definition. On this interpretation a miracle must not only be a physical event which would never have occurred except through the action of a transcendent rational agent, but also an event that clearly has religious significance and is of such an extraordinary nature it is either directly perceived as a miracle or immediately inferred as such. This understanding of the term insists that "the qualia of the miraculous is of such a nature as to strongly and clearly suggest to the human mind the presence of the supernatural."[10]

In my view, this latter treatment is more accurate and precise. It enables us to distinguish between events which, although they would not have occurred except through the action of an agent who transcends nature, need not necessarily be so interpreted, such as a freely willed action on the part of a human agent[11] and physical events which strongly and clearly suggest the presence of an agent who transcends nature, such as the turning of water into wine or walking on water. It also enables us to distinguish between events which, although they strongly suggest the presence of a transcendent agent, have little or no religious significance (poltergeist activity, say) and events which not only suggest the presence of a transcendent agent but also have great religious significance (the resurrection of Christ, for example).

I wish to emphasize that I am not arguing that it is always easy to attach a precise meaning to the term *religiously significant*. Neither am I arguing that it is always easy to decide into which category a particular event fits. What I am arguing is that, although there may exist borderline cases, we must distinguish between three types of physical events caused by transcendent agents. These are: (1) events which, although they might have occurred through the action of an agent who transcends nature, are not either directly perceived or immediately inferred as such; (2) events which, although they strongly suggest the activity of a transcendent agent, have little or no religious significance; and (3) events which strongly and clearly suggest the activity of a transcendent agent and which have religious significance.

In the interests of clarity, I suggest that we ought to reserve the term *miracle* for this last category of physical events. This, of course, is not to say that these other two types of event are of little importance or theoretical interest. It is merely to draw some useful distinctions.

By way of illustrating how important it is to make these distinctions, I want briefly to examine the notion of "false" miracles, a topic not much discussed these days but of considerable interest to earlier thinkers. Both the Old Testament and New Testament recognize a class of events which involve the overriding of nature by transcendent agents, but to which they evince a negative attitude. Thus Jesus warns his followers of false prophets capable of performing great signs and portents which might deceive even the elect (Matthew 24:24).

In this passage and others, even before the concept of a miracle has been elaborated with philosophical rigour and exactness, we find recognized the fact that a genuine miracle is not merely an overriding of nature, but an overriding of nature that is in accord with God's purposes. We find also a sensitivity to the fact that overridings of nature might be produced by transcendent agents who are in opposition to God's will and that it may not always be easy, at least in the short term, to decide which overridings are in accord with God's will, and hence genuine miracles. This passage shows that, however difficult it may be to decide on whether an event is religiously significant, we betray a poor understanding of the concept of a miracle if we focus on the fact that it constitutes an overriding of nature and neglect the question of how it can be seen to fulfil God's purposes.

A miracle, then, is an unusual and religiously significant event beyond the power of nature to produce and caused by an agent who transcends nature. Most philosophers, however, would insist that this definition is incomplete. They would want to add the further requirement that a miracle must be understood as being, in some sense, a violation of the laws of nature. I think their reason for wanting to add this further requirement is that they think that if a miracle is conceived as an event which would not have occurred were nature left to its own devices then this implies that a miracle cannot occur without violating some law of nature.

Although this view that a miracle must violate some law of nature is commonly accepted, I think it is mistaken. So brash and ambitious a claim on my part needs considerable defence and this is one of the central projects of my subsequent chapters. For now, I wish only to observe that it is not immediately obvious that a miracle must be conceived as violating the laws of nature. The idea of violation forms no part of the defintion of a miracle, but is presumed to be implied by the definition. Whether this presumption is justified deserves careful scrutiny, especially in light of the fact that many of our difficulties with the concept stem from the view that miracles must be conceived as violations. If it should turn out that they need not be conceived as violating the laws of nature then it may well emerge, as I remarked earlier, that we have caused ourselves needless philosophical difficulty by not being careful enough in excluding extraneous elements from our definition.

CHAPTER TWO

Miracles and the Laws of Nature

As I have remarked, miracles are usually at least partially defined as violations of the laws of nature. The consequences of defining them in this way are important. The view that some of nature's laws must be violated if a transcendent agent overrides the usual course of events has led many philosophers to say that the evidence in favour of a miracle must inevitably conflict with the evidence in favour of the laws of nature. It has led others to go further and suggest that the idea of miracles is a mere pseudo-concept. For example, Flew has suggested that there is something logically scandalous about the idea of a law of nature being violated.[1] He claims that the idea is self-contradictory inasmuch as the laws of nature must be conceived as exceptionless. He contends that scientists use the term *law of nature* in such a way that "if something occurs inconsistent with some proposition previously believed to express ... a law [of nature], this occurrence is, not an occasion for proclaiming a miraculous violation, but as a reason for confessing the error of the former belief, and for resolving to search for the law which does hold."[2]

Those who have attempted to defend the concept of miracle have generally accepted the view that a miracle violates the laws of nature and that any evidence in favour of a miracle must, therefore, inevitably conflict with the evidence in favour of the laws of nature. They have attempted to show that it is nevertheless conceivable that there could exist sufficient evidence to justify belief in miracles. In reply to stronger claims that it is not logically possible that a law of nature could be violated, they have argued that we can make sense of the notion of a non-repeatable counter-instance to a law of nature. Douglas Odegard, for example, argues that, even if a miracle implies that the laws of nature have been violated, a case can be made for thinking they are possible, detectable, and compatible with science. He suggests that all that is required is that we define law-violations as events of a kind that is epistemically impossible, unless there is good evidence of a god's producing an instance.[3] Implicit in this suggestion is the idea that we may build boundary conditions into the laws of nature that specify under what circumstances they hold. In a similar vein, Swinburne claims that

to say a certain ... formula is a law is to say that in general its predictions are true and that any exceptions to its operations cannot be accounted for by another formula which could be taken as a law ... [We] must ... distinguish between a formula being a law and a formula being (universally) true or being a law which holds without exception.[4]

My view is that the assumption upon which this debate is founded is erroneous. I think the idea that miracles can occur only if the laws of nature are violated is false. I will argue that it is entirely conceivable that miracles can occur in a world which behaves, always and everywhere, completely in accordance with the laws of nature. Establishing this will allow me to demonstrate that the standard assumption that evidence in favour of miracles must conflict with the evidence for the laws of nature is false, and to dismiss as irrelevant the question of whether it makes sense to talk of violations of the laws of nature. I turn to the task of defending my view.

MIRACLES AND THE LAWS OF NATURE

Let me begin by saying what I understand by the term *law of nature*. I take it to refer to a scientific law which is in fact true. I hasten to add that by scientific law I do not mean a mere "inductive generalization" or "experimental law." Rather, I refer to the theoretical laws or principles which serve to explain the experimental laws and general regularities discovered by scientists. On my view, although the term *law of nature* refers to a universal conditional that may in principle be confirmed or disconfirmed on the basis of empirical evidence, this conditional will contain terms which refer not directly to observed regularities, but to unobservable entities and properties (for example, electrons), which serve to explain the observed regularities. Thus the laws of nature cannot be directly confirmed or disconfirmed by observation, but must be indirectly confirmed or disconfirmed through predictions made on their basis.

Having indicated how I am using the term *law of nature*, I wish to note a commonplace feature of scientific explanation, namely that it has the following form:

$(C_1 \ldots C_n)$,
$(L_1 \ldots L_m)$,
therefore E,

where $(C_1 \ldots C_n)$, is a set of singular statements describing relevant initial conditions, and where $(L_1 \ldots L_m)$ is a set of general laws, and where E, the event to be explained, is a logical consequence of the Cs and Ls but not the Cs alone. As is well known, the same schema can be used to predict the occurrence of E if $(C_1 \ldots C_n)$ were to occur.

We may, I think, leave aside the complicated discussion of whether the laws of nature are best conceived as absolute or statistical.[5] The point that I want to emphasize is this. Although we often speak as though the laws of nature are sufficient to explain the occurrence of an event, this is not really so. Inasmuch as they are merely conditionals, the laws cannot by themselves explain the occurrence of any event.[6] What this means is that a scientific explanation must not only make reference to the laws of nature, but also to the actual "stuff" of nature, the matter or, more accurately, mass / energy, whose behaviour is described by the laws.

If we keep in mind this basic distinction between the laws of nature and the "stuff" whose behaviour they describe, we can see that, although a miracle is an event which never would have occurred had not nature been over-ridden, and although the notion of a miracle is logically dependent upon the notion of a known order to which it constitutes an exception, this in no way entails that a miracle must violate the laws of nature. The reason this is true is this. If God creates or annihilates a unit or units of mass / energy He breaks no law of nature, but He does, by the creation of new mass / energy, or by the annihilation of previously existing mass / energy, change the material conditions to which the laws of nature apply. He would thereby produce an event which nature on its own would not have produced.

It is important to emphasize that the occurrence of such an event would in no way imply that the laws of nature had been contravened. We do not, for example, violate the laws of motion if we toss an extra billiard ball into a group of billiard balls in motion on a billiard table. There is no moment at which the laws of motion are contravened. What we do by introducing the extra billiard ball is change the material conditions to which the laws of motion apply and hence change the result which would otherwise be expected. Similarly, by creating or annihilating a unit or units of mass / energy, God may produce in nature an event that could not otherwise occur without violating the laws of nature.

To anticipate an objection, it will not do to argue that if a miracle occurs then some instance of the implication of the complete set of laws of nature is contravened, and therefore, by *modus tollens*, at least one of the laws in the set is contravened. Put somewhat differently, it will not do to argue that if a miracle is an exception to the regular course of nature, then it is *ipso facto* an exception to some law, since the complete set of laws entails a complete description of the course of nature. Such an argument fails to take into account the fact that the complete set of laws entails the complete description of the course of nature only if the material conditions to which the laws apply are not changed. To revert to our billiard table example, the laws of motion entail the description of the action of the billiard balls only so long as no extra balls are introduced into the system. Similarly, the complete set of the laws of nature entails a complete description of the course of nature only so long as God does not create or annihilate mass / energy, thus changing the material conditions to which the laws apply.

I think there are two objections that might be raised against this argument. The first is that its conclusion can only be reached by offering an arbitrary definition of the term *law of nature*. The second is that, even if it be granted that the definition put forward is adequate, the argument still implies that at least one law of nature must be violated if a miracle occurs, since the creation or annihilation of mass / energy implies that the First Law of Thermodynamics has been violated.

Considering the first objection, I suppose it might be urged by a critic that the term *law of nature* is best understood as meaning merely a well-established regularity of nature. For example, the critic might maintain that it is a law of nature that virgins do not give birth. Presumably, if the miracle of the Virgin Birth actually occurred then the law of nature that virgins do not give birth must have been violated.

If we grant the critic this definition then it seems to

follow that a miracle is indeed a violation of the laws of nature. Unfortunately for the critic, it follows that a number of non-miraculous events which we are not normally inclined to view as being violations of the laws of nature must also be classed as violations of these laws. Consider the possible case of a virgin who, through surgical procedures, has a fertilized egg implanted in her uterus. After a period of nine months this woman gives birth. Although we might find such an event unusual, we would scarcely be inclined to view it as violating the laws of nature. Regularities in nature, such as the fact that virgins do not usually give birth, may be explicable by reference to the laws of nature, but it does not seem plausible to view them as being themselves laws of nature.

The critic might argue that this distinction does not fully resolve the difficulty. Granted that we must distinguish between the laws of nature and well-established regularity of nature, we are nevertheless firmly convinced that there are a great number of well-established regularities of nature which, in the absence of extraordinary circumstances, admit of no exceptions. Surely the regularity of nature that, in the normal course of events, virgins do not give birth admits of no exceptions.

The claim that we are firmly and justifiably convinced that, all other things being equal, some regularities of nature admit of no exceptions can scarcely be denied. It must also be granted that our conviction that virgins do not, in the usual course of events, give birth falls into this category. However, what must be emphasized is that it is precisely the contention of the believer in a miracle that all other things were not equal. Thus those who believe in the miracle of the Virgin Birth hold that this event is, in some respects, analogous to the hypothetical case of the virgin who through surgical procedures had a fertilized egg implanted in her uterus. They are analogous not in the means by which the result of a virgin birth is achieved, but in that in neither case are "all other things equal." In our hypothetical case a human agent, that is, the surgeon, intervenes so as to change the material situation to which the laws of nature apply. In the case of the Virgin Birth, a divine agent, that is, God, intervenes so as to change the material situation to which the laws of nature apply. Both produce in nature an event which would not otherwise occur and which constitutes an exception to a well-established regularity of nature. In neither case are "all other things equal" and in neither case is there any reason to suppose that the laws of nature must be violated in order for the event to occur.

My argument, then, is that miracles are, in an important sense, analogous to acts of human agents. Thus, if a human agent may act in such a way as to produce an exception to a regularity of nature which in the absence of action on the part of some agent would admit of no exception, it seems reasonable to suppose that a divine agent might act similarly. It follows that if a human agent need not violate any laws of nature in producing an event which is an exception to a well-established regularity of nature then neither need a divine agent violate any laws of nature in producing such an event.

The critic might reply that I have not made miracles easier to conceive so much as raised problems concerning the notion of agency. If the notion of agency implies that agents in some significant way stand outside physical processes, yet act in such a way as to influence physical processes, this suggests that interactionism is a correct theory of the mind-body relation. Surely such a theory of mind-body interaction is difficult to defend.

The critic is quite right to suggest that, in the final analysis, the question of miracles cannot be considered in isolation from a number of other important philosophical issues. There are links between the concept of miracles and the mind-body problem and, while I do not propose to set forth my position on this latter issue, it is my view that ordinary human actions no less than miracles disconfirm physicalism. Although I do not intend in this work to develop a general theory of agency and show its relation to mind-body interaction and the issue of miracles, it is nevertheless appropriate to note that even if the idea of agency I have employed implies the truth of some version of interactionism, it is not usually objected that the interaction of mind and body implies that the laws of nature are violated.

True, it is sometimes objected that the interaction of mind and body would violate the First Law of Thermodynamics in that the action of an immaterial mind upon a physical body apparently implies the nonconservation of energy. However, this is only to urge against mind-body interaction the second objection to my argument that miracles do not imply the violation of the laws of nature and to demonstrate that there are important conceptual links between the mind-body problem and the issue of miracles. It is to this second objection that I wish now to proceed.

Prima facie, this second objection seems much harder to deal with than the first. There seems no way around the conclusion that if a miracle involves either the creation or annihilation of mass / energy then the occurrence of a miracle implies that the law known as the First Law of Thermodynamics (the Principle of the Conservation of Energy) has been violated. I shall show that this difficulty is apparent rather than real.

The answer to this objection lies in a hitherto unnoticed distinction which must be made between two forms of the Principle of the Conservation of Energy. This Principle is commonly stated as "Energy can neither be created nor destroyed, although its form may change" or as "In an isolated system [that is, a system not causally influenced by something other than itself] the total amount of energy remains constant, although its form may change."

These two formulations are used interchangeably, the unspoken assumption being that they are logically equivalent. It is important, however, to realize that they are not. We can deduce from the proposition "Energy can neither be created nor destroyed" the proposition "In an isolated system the total amount of energy remains constant." We cannot from the proposition "In an isolated system the total amount of energy remains constant" deduce the statement "Energy can neither be created nor destroyed."

This reveals that the proposition "Energy can neither be created nor destroyed" is considerably stronger than the proposition "In an isolated system the total amount of energy remains constant." The former proposition could not be held by a theist, since this claim by definition rules out the possibility of creation *ex nihilo*. By contrast, a theist could hold that in an isolated system – a system not subject to the causal influence of something other than itself – energy remains constant, since this claim implies nothing concerning the possibility of creation *ex nihilo*, just as it implies nothing concerning whether in fact the universe is an isolated system or open to reordering by a transcendent agent.

The critic might be tempted to suggest that I am begging an important question. She might suggest that if we postulate that God created the universe together with all its natural laws then there is no reason to think that theism is incompatible with the strong form of the Principle. Surely it is not, unless we assume that miracles occur. To assume that theism and the strong form of the Principle are incompatible amounts, therefore, to special pleading for the existence of miracles.

What such an objection fails to take into account is that the strong form of the Principle not only rules out miracles, but any notion of God creating the universe. Once we accept the claim that energy can neither be created nor destroyed, it makes no sense to talk of God creating the universe, since the universe, being composed of different forms of energy, must be conceived as *uncreated* and indestructible. To say that the universe is uncreated and indestructible amounts to saying that it does not depend for its being upon God, and this is a claim which is incompatible with the truth of theism. The critic, then, is simply wrong if she asserts that the strong form of the Principle is compatible with theism.

I wish to emphasize two points about the possibility of drawing this distinction between the two forms of the Principle. First, the person who believes in miracles is under no compulsion to deny what I have called the weak form of the Principle. He rejects not the well-evidenced claim that in a causally isolated system energy is conserved, but the much weaker claim that nature is an isolated system in the sense that it is not open to the causal influence of God. Of course, he must deny what I have called the strong form of the Principle, namely the claim that energy can neither be created nor destroyed. However, this should not bother him overmuch, since the strong form *a priori* rules out the possibility of theism being true.

Second, it may prove possible for the believer in miracles to accept the weak form of the Principle and yet deny the legitimacy of the inference required to arrive at its strong form. *Prima facie* at least, the believer is not being absurd if she accepts the claim that "in an isolated system the total amount of energy remains constant," but denies the legitimacy of the further inference that "Energy can neither be created nor destroyed." If this inference can be blocked the believer will be in a position to accept all the experimental evidence which is taken to support the Principle of the Conservation of Energy, since our actual experimental evidence only demonstrates that in a causally isolated system the total amount of energy remains constant. In short, she will be in a position to affirm the Principle of the Conservation of Energy when it is formulated as a scientific law and not as an *a priori* metaphysical principle which excludes the possibility of theism being true.

Whether this inference can be blocked is an important question that will concern us in later chapters; I shall argue that it can be. Here I wish only to emphasize that, providing she can block the inference required to move from the weak to the strong form of the Principle, the believer may claim that miracles need not be conceived as violating any law of nature.

It should be noted that this conclusion only follows if it is appropriate to view miracles as events which are at least partially caused by an act of creation or annihilation of mass / energy. I say "at least partially" because it is clear that the event which is termed a miracle may be a product of both the already functioning processes of nature and an act of creation or annihilation. For example, the miracle of the Virgin Birth can be seen as an event in which an act of creation by God (the creation of a spermatozoon in the body of Mary), combined with existent natural processes (the normal growth and development of a fetus during pregnancy), to produce the miraculous event we call the Virgin Birth. Or, to develop a different example in which the annihilation of mass / energy could have played a part, certain acts of healing on Christ's part might have involved the annihilation of material making up harmful tumours or infections. Or, to take this line of thought a step further, it is entirely possible that a miracle might involve both acts of creation and acts of annihilation. Christ's healing of lepers might have involved both the annihilation of diseased cells and the creation of new tissue to replace that previously lost to the disease.

In all of these instances it seems clear that an act of creation or annihilation could combine with already functioning natural processes to produce the event we call a miracle. It should be emphasized on the other hand that a miracle need not have prior natural processes linked to it; the miracle of the multiplication of loaves and fishes appears to have been a direct act of creation in which already functioning natural processes played little or no part.

It may be objected that, while some miracles can plausibly be seen as involving creation or annihilation of energy, it is not possible to explain other miracles in this way. The Virgin Birth, the healing miracles, the multiplication of the loaves and fishes are all quite easily explained on my account, but what of Jesus walking on the water, the raising of Lazarus, and the Resurrection?

However, the objection is not well-founded. I see no reason for thinking that this latter class of miracles is any more difficult to explain in terms of the creation or the annihilation of energy than the first. Concerning Jesus walking on water, there is no question that if the right amount of force is exerted at the right spatio-temporal co-ordinates it is possible for a physical body to move across the surface of water, even though its density is greater than that of the water. The example may seem ridiculous, but it might be noted that a man with a jet pack may move about in the air even though he is heavier than air. He does so by generating force and using it to counter the effect of certain other forces. My point is not that Jesus must have had access to advanced technology, but that if he could, by the creation of energy, generate force it was not in principle impossible for him to walk across the surface of water. All that is required is the right balance of forces and there is no doubt that this could be achieved if one had the ability to create or annihilate the very stuff of nature. The raising of Lazarus seems no more difficult a case. Death is invariably the result of some dysfunctioning of the body. Given the ability to create or annihilate units of mass / energy, I see no reason why Jesus could not have repaired and reversed the effects of such dysfunction, thus restoring Lazarus to life. Even though the event was more dramatic than some of his other miracles, the processes involved need not have differed essentially from any of his other healing miracles. Neither is it impossible to explain the Resurrection. It seems entirely conceivable that after Jesus' death God might have reversed the damage done to the body, thus bringing it to life. We might also postulate that, after his Resurrection, Jesus was able by his creative power to alter his body at will, perhaps even assembling or disassembling it on occasion.[7] This would explain a number of puzzling aspects of his Resurrection appearances, such as his ability to appear suddenly in a locked room.

Put more generally, my point is this. All physical events, including miracles, can be described in terms of a certain amount and ordering of energy. If the event can be conceived then so can that particular amount and ordering of energy. Thus, for any miracle, it would always be possible for a transcendent agent to produce it by the creation or annihilation of energy, since all that is required is that the agent bring about the particular amount and ordering of energy necessary for the miracle.

The critic might also argue that my account has no advantage over the traditional account when it comes to observing the occurrence of a miracle. Miracles still constitute an exception to the usual course of nature on both accounts, and however we conceive them, miracles continue to look like violations of the laws of nature. This in turn seems to imply that no answer can be given to the question of why we should regard an unusual event as a miracle and not just an index of our inadequate understanding of the laws of nature.

Again, I think the objection is weak. In insisting that my account of a miracle must not only be conceptually distinct from traditional violation accounts, but also observationally distinct, the critic conflates two related but different questions. My view that a miracle need not be understood as a violation of the laws of nature concerns the ontological question of how best to define a miracle. It does not address the epistemological question of how we recognize a miracle or distinguish it from other unusual, but nevertheless natural, events. It is true that my view has epistemological implications, but these concern the amount of evidence needed to establish the occurrence of a miracle, not the criteria by which we judge whether an event is a miracle.

In other words, I would maintain that we must distinguish between the question of how much evidence is needed to establish the occurrence of a miracle and the question of what the best interpretation of an unusual event is. My argument that a miracle need not violate the laws of nature bears on the first issue and not the second. Thus, although the critic is quite right to point out that my argument is incapable of generating criteria by which a miracle can be distinguished from unusual but non-miraculous events, she errs in thinking that I attempt to use it for this purpose. My aim is not to generate criteria, but to say something about the amount of evidence required to establish a miracle's occurrence. I do not deny that the question of criteria is an important one and the reader will find that I have a good deal to say about it in my discussion in chapter four of Guy Robinson's position. It is a mistake, however, to think that my present argument must also bear on the question of criteria, at least in the direct way that the critic demands.

It seems promising, then, to think of miracles not as conflicting with the laws of nature, but as involving acts of creation or annihilation of that to which the laws apply. By annihilating or creating units of mass / energy and so changing the material conditions to which the laws of nature apply, God could produce within nature events which nature would not otherwise produce. With the possible exception of the First Law of Thermodynamics (the Principle of the Conservation of Energy) such events would not imply that any of the laws of nature had been violated. [8]

CHAPTER THREE

David Hume and Prior Probability

It is time to consider some philosophical objections to belief in miracles. In this chapter I shall examine David Hume's famous "balance-of-probabilities" argument found in Part I of his essay "Of Miracles." I shall be proposing what might be described as the traditional interpretation of Hume's position. It has been subject to much criticism recently; some preliminary remarks are therefore in order.

TWO INTERPRETATIONS OF HUME'S ESSAY

Traditionally, Hume has been taken as putting forth an argument that no amount or quality of testimonial evidence could ever justify the conclusion that a miracle did in fact occur. Antony Flew has challenged this view recently, arguing that Hume intended only to demonstrate that there must exist "peculiar and important difficulties inherent in any attempt to establish that a genuinely miraculous event did in fact occur."[1] Contrary to the traditional view, Flew feels that the argument "allows the theoretical possibility of establishing that a miraculous event has occurred."[2]

By way of supporting this view, Flew appeals to several features of the text. He notes that in the second paragraph of the essay Hume speaks of the argument as merely a check to belief. He also quotes extensively from Hume's last three paragraphs in Part I of the essay and the first paragraph of Part II, where Hume's language seems to suggest the possibility of there being sufficient testimonial evidence to establish belief in miracles. Finally, he appeals to the fact that in Part II of the essay Hume argues that the actual evidence in favour of miracles is very poor. The existence of Part II, he argues, indicates that Hume did not understand his argument in Part I to preclude the theoretical possibility that belief in miracles might be justified on the basis of testimonial evidence, and thus felt compelled to bolster his case by adding some further arguments.

Suggestive though it is, I do not think Flew's reading can be sustained. In the second paragraph of the essay Hume writes:

Nothing is so convenient as a decisive argument of this kind, which must at least silence the most arrogant bigotry and superstition and free us from their impertinent solicitations. I flatter myself that I have discovered an argument of a like nature which, if just, will, with the wise and learned, be an everlasting check to all kinds of superstitious delusion, and consequently will be useful as long as the world endures; for so long, I presume, will the accounts of miracles and prodigies be found in all history, sacred and profane.[3]

Flew thinks that Hume explicitly limits the claims he makes for his argument, but it seems clear that Hume is writing ironically. Flew himself stresses that the introductory paragraph of the essay is "mischievously modest" and this tone certainly continues at the beginning of the second. It therefore seems more reasonable to interpret Hume's use of the word "check" and the phrase "must at least silence" as deliberate and bantering understatement of the force of the argument and not a serious classification of it as merely defensive. This interpretation is further strengthened when we take into account Hume's use of a number of words and phrases upon which Flew omits comment. As R.M. Burns notes, the use of phrases such as "decisive," "silence," "free us," "everlasting check to all kinds," and "as long as the world endure" indicate not so much a defensive attitude as an aggressive certitude. [4]

Concerning the last three paragraphs of Part I and the first paragraph of Part II from which Flew quotes so extensively, it must be admitted that, considered in isolation from the rest of the essay, they seem to offer some support for his view. However, to interpret them in this manner is to ignore the possibility that Hume at this point, as he so often does, is writing ironically. Certainly his talk of weighing miracle against miracle is difficult to take literally. It seems more likely designed to emphasize that belief in miracles is intrinsically absurd. As Burns puts it, "Hume should ... be regarded as suggesting through use of extravagant language that there is something ridiculously paradoxical about belief in miracles." [5] This conclusion is strengthened when we note that Hume asserts in the second of these paragraphs both that "the proof against a miracle ... is as entire as any argument from experience can possibly be imagined" [6] and that a "miracle [can only be] rendered credible ... by an opposite proof which is superior." [7] He can scarcely have failed to realize that asserting both these propositions does not leave open the possibility of establishing the occurrence of miracles, since taken together they imply that no testimony could ever be sufficiently strong to establish belief in a miracle.

Flew seems on firmer ground when he claims that his reading of the text provides a better explanation of Part II of the essay than does the traditional view. Several points need to be noted, however. First, scattered throughout Part II are a number of comments which can only be interpreted as references to the argument of Part I understood according to the classical interpretation. [8] For example, we find him writing in Part II "that ... [it is] not requisite, in order to reject a fact of this nature [a miracle], to be able accurately to disprove the testimony ... a miracle, supported by any human testimony, ... [is] more properly a subject of derision than of argument."[9] Second, it is worth noting that the classical interpretation was the one adopted in all the responses made to the argument during Hume's lifetime and Hume never raised any objection to this reading of his argument.[10] This is surely strange if he felt that his critics had fundamentally misunderstood the argument. Finally, it is significant that Hume took great pride in the argument found in Part I, this pride being based on his belief in its decisiveness and originality. If Flew's reading is accepted, it is a mystery how Hume could ever think this. He would certainly be aware that no argument which acknowledges the theoretical possibility of miracles could ever be entirely decisive. He would also be aware that orthodox apologists generally granted his point that the testimonial evidence needed to justify a miracle must be of a higher quality than that needed to establish a non-miraculous event.

My conclusion is that Flew's interpretation cannot be adopted. I wish to emphasize that this is not to suggest there are not elements in the essay which point in the direction of Flew's view; they are, however, much more fitful and sporadic than Flew recognizes. On the whole, the traditional interpretation is more satisfactory and more clearly reflects Hume's thought. The very most that Hume is prepared to allow is that there might conceivably be a case where one might have to suspend both belief and disbelief. Contrary to Flew's interpretation, he does not allow as a theoretical possibility that the evidence for a miracle could outweigh the evidence against a miracle.

HUME'S "BALANCE-OF-PROBABILITIES" ARGUMENT

Hume's argument found in Part I of the essay is this:

1 Experience is our "only guide in reasoning concerning matters of fact." (115)

2 "It must be acknowledged that this guide [experience] is not altogether infallible but in some cases is apt to lead us into errors."(115)

3 Therefore, "a wise man ... proportions his belief to the evidence. In such conclusions as are founded on an infallible experience, he expects the event with the last degree of assurance and regards his past experience as a full proof of the future existence of that event. In other cases he proceeds with more caution; he weighs the opposite experiments; he considers which side is supported by the greater number of experiments – to that side he inclines with doubt and hestitation; and when at last he fixes his judgment the evidence exceeds not what we properly call 'probability.' " (116)

4 "We ought not to make an exception to this principle in favour of human testimony." (117)

5 "We do not have a firm and unalterable experience that human testimony is always trustworthy." (123)

6 "A firm and unalterable experience has established the laws of nature." (119)

7 "A miracle is a violation of the laws of nature." (119)

8 Therefore, since "a uniform experience amounts to a proof, there is ... a direct and full proof from the nature of the fact, against the existence of any miracle, nor can such a proof be destroyed or the miracle rendered credible but by an opposite proof which is superior." (120)

9 "The proof against a miracle from the very nature of the fact, is as entire as any argument from experience can possibly be imagined." (119)

10 Therefore, "no testimony is sufficient to establish a miracle unless the testimony be of such a kind that its falsehood would be more miraculous than the fact which it endeavours to establish." (120)

SOME CRITICISMS OF HUME'S ARGUMENT

A number of criticisms have been made of this argument. First, it is worth noting that Hume's treatment of miracles is inconsistent with his treatment of induction and causality. In his treatment of induction he says that the move from regular experience of event A followed by event B to the belief that event A will invariably be followed by event B is logically unjustified. Presumably such belief is merely the result of a strong psychological tendency to believe in uniformity. We may speak, therefore, of two psychological tendencies: the tendency of certain people to believe in absolute uniformity and the tendency of others to believe in miracles. As psychological states these two beliefs are on equal footing and Hume does not give, and on his own theory is unable to give, any reason for preferring one belief to the other.

Equally, if his analysis of causation be accepted, namely that there exist no necessary connections between events, his discussion of whether or not it is rational to believe a report of a miracle begs the question. As Flew admits, "to dismiss out of hand all testimony to the occurrence beyond the range of our observations of a counter example, on the sole ground that such an occurrence would falsify the universal generalization based upon our observations to date would be arbitrary and bigotted."[11]

Hume should have either repudiated his explicitly stated position concerning induction and causality or else admitted that his conception of what is meant by a law of nature prohibited him from pressing his objection to miracles. If a law of nature is nothing more than a strong psychological tendency to believe in uniformity it can hardly be a legitimate reason for rejecting reports of non-uniform events such as miracles.

A second criticism which can be made of the argument is that it commits us to maintaining that no event is a miracle unless it is absolutely unique. The claim that a miracle must contradict the whole course of experience is an untenable one. Surely, despite the fact that Elijah is reported to have multiplied food, Christ's multiplication of the loaves and fishes has to be judged miraculous.[12] As C.D. Broad comments, "It seems arbitrary to suppose that two or three exceptions to a regularity necessarily prove that it is not a law of nature and consequently that none of the exceptions are miraculous."[13] If he is to be consistent, Hume is forced to say just this. Clearly, he overemphasizes the fact that a miracle is a non-uniform event to the neglect of the fact that it is an event caused by a rational agent who transcends nature.

Third, Hume seems guilty of trying to decide a factual matter by definitional gymnastics. He states that the concept of a miracle is not self-contradictory and that it is logically possible that miracles might occur. This seems to imply that whether in fact they do is a matter for empirical investigation. He does not think this is so, however. His argument is designed to show there is no need for investigation. It amounts to the claim that, simply by analysing the concept of miracle and the way in which belief in miracles would have to be established, and the concept of natural law and the way in which belief in the laws of nature must be established, we can come to the realization that there could never exist sufficient evidence to justify belief miracles.

But this commits him to an untenable view. He is quite emphatic that evidence can count against reports of miracles. To say this is to admit that miracles, if they occur, are recognizable events, since otherwise we would have no idea of what we render improbable by presenting contrary evidence. So far so good; this is exactly what we would expect if we must resolve the issue by empirical investigation. However, he goes on to assert that we could never have sufficient positive evidence to justify belief in miracles. It is this move which is questionable. It commits him to holding that there are logically possible empirical events which no conceivable amount of positive evidence could ever confirm, but which a finite body of negative evidence disconfirms. In other words, miracles are logically possible, and empirical evidence is relevant to establishing whether they actually occur, but there could not, even in principle, exist sufficient positive evidence to justify belief in their occurrence. [14]

Given this conclusion, one may be pardoned for thinking the argument has gone wrong somewhere. Exactly where is an issue I take up in the next section of this chapter. For now, all I shall say is that Hume has erred in defining a miracle and that this is what leads to difficulties.

Fourth, and finally, his argument proves too much. It not only prohibits belief in reports of miracles, but also progress in science. Belief in the laws of nature, no less than belief in miracles, rests mainly on testimonial evidence. Moreover, there have been many statements held to express natural laws because of an invariable experience in their favour which, upon later observation of exceptions, were subsequently abandoned. If Hume's argument is accepted, this procedure must be judged irrational, since the first reported exception, to anyone who has not observed it, occupies the same logical status as the report of a miracle. Thus,

those ... to whom the first exception was reported ought to have rejected it, and gone on believing in the alleged law of nature. Yet, if the report of the first exception makes no difference to their belief in the law, their state of belief will be precisely the same when a second exception is reported as it was on the first occasion. Hence if the first report ought to make no difference to their belief in the law, neither ought the second. So that it would seem on Hume's theory that if, up to a certain time, I and every one else have always observed A to be followed by B then no amount of testimony from the most trustworthy persons that they have observed A not followed by B ought to have the least effect on my belief in the law.[15]

That Hume was not unaware of this objection can, perhaps, be inferred from his discussion of people in a warm climate who, having never directly observed that water freezes, are told that water freezes. He comments:

it must be confessed that, in the present case of freezing, the event follows contrary to the rules of analogy and is such as a rational Indian would not look for. The operations of cold upon water are not gradual, according to the degrees of cold; but whenever it comes to the freezing point the water passes in a moment from the utmost liquidity to perfect hardness. Such an event, therefore, may be denominated "extraordinary" and requires a pretty strong testimony to render it credible to people in a warm climate: but still it is not miraculous, nor contrary to uniform experience of the course of nature in cases where all the circumstances are the same.[16]

Judging from this passage, his reply is that strong testimony constitutes sufficient grounds to establish belief in "unusual" events beyond the ken of one's experience so long as the reports of such events also indicate that the circumstances under which the events took place were somewhat foreign to one's experience.

This response seems inadequate. It ignores the fact that the "people who discover exceptions to alleged general laws are seldom the same people who explain them."[17] For example, it often happens that a researcher reports an exception to an alleged general law even though he cannot identify any relevant background circumstance that is even subtly different from those under which more usual results are obtained. Unless suitably strong testimony establishes at least a provisional belief in the occurrence of the event, the theoretician has no reason to think there is anything that needs explanation or investigation.

It might be replied that this belief is only provisional, that if only one researcher reports an exception, and if the theoretician upon careful inspection of the report of the conditions under which the reported exception occurred can find no relevant background condition that could serve to explain or make plausible the unusual results, then he would be justified in concluding that the apparent exception never occurred.

Suppose, though, that a significant minority of reputable, independent researchers report that they on occasion obtain similar results. Surely it is possible to imagine conditions under which it would be irrational to dismiss the reports of exceptions even though it is as yet impossible to point to any relevant differing background condition that is different from those under which more usual results are obtained. If it is to progress, science must admit the possibility of such exceptions to alleged general laws, since otherwise there is no need to think there is anything that needs explanation and consequently no need to revise scientific theory. Inasmuch as it precludes this typical activity on the part of scientists, Hume's argument not only rules out belief in miracles, but the possibility of progress in science.

AN ALTERNATIVE APPROACH TO HUME'S "BALANCE-OF-PROBABILITIES" ARGUMENT

All the criticisms discussed in the preceding section are important and go a long way toward showing there is something wrong with Hume's famous argument. They leave us, however, with the uneasy feeling that the matter has not been fully resolved. Despite the fact that we cannot rule out the possibility of there being sufficient testimonial evidence to justify belief in miracles, we are left with the feeling that there exists a certain irresolvable tension between reports of miracle and belief in the laws of nature.

This, I think, is a consequence of the way the argument has been criticized. The argument may be summarized as follows:

1 The testimonial evidence in favour of a miracle inevitably conflicts with the evidence in favour of laws of nature.

2 The testimonial evidence in favour of a miracle cannot exceed, even in principle, the evidence in favour of laws of nature.

3 Therefore, belief in the occurrence of a miracle can never be justified on the grounds of testimonial evidence.

Critics have focused their attention entirely upon the second premise. Unreflectively accepting Hume's claim that the testimonial evidence in favour of miracles inevitably conflicts with the evidence in favour of laws of nature, they have left the first premise unexamined. However, accepting the first premise means that, even if there is evidence which justifies belief in a miracle, this evidence must necessarily conflict with another body of evidence we are strongly inclined to accept, namely the evidence which justifies belief in the laws of nature. As Hume says:

The very same principle of experience which gives us a certain degree of assurance in the testimony of witnesses gives us also, in this case [reports of miracles], another degree of assurance against the fact which they endeavour to establish: from which contradiction there necessarily arises a counterpoise and mutual destruction of belief and authority.[18]

The truth of this premise must be questioned, however. It depends for its plausibility upon the assumption that if a miracle is an event which nature could not have produced on its own then it must violate the laws of nature. As I have shown in chapter two, this assumption is suspect. Arguably, miracles need violate no laws of nature. If this be true, then the testimonial evidence in favour of miracles need not be conceived as conflicting with the evidence which grounds belief in the laws of nature, and Hume's "balance-of-probabilities" argument cannot even get started.

This means that the distinction I drew in chapter two between the strong and the weak form of the Principle of the Conservation of Energy is especially important. Whether or not a miracle need be conceived as violating a law of nature, and hence whether the evidence in favour of a miracle need be conceived as conflicting with the evidence supporting belief in the laws of nature, will depend upon whether the strong form of the Principle is best conceived as well-evidenced law of nature or a questionable metaphysical assumption.

Questions, then, of how the strong form of the Principle is best conceived and of its relation to the experimental evidence that grounds belief in the weak form of the Principle are of considerable importance. I propose to address these questions, but only after I have discussed some contemporary objections that are often raised against belief in miracles. Here, I only wish to stress that, unless the strong form of the Principle can be justified, it makes no sense to assume that the evidence in favour of a miracle conflicts with the evidence that grounds belief in the laws of nature.

CHAPTER FOUR

Further Objections to Miracles

Hume's *a priori* argument in Part I of his essay is perhaps the best known criticism of belief in miracles. Other important arguments have been advanced in recent analytical philosophy, however, to show that, for various conceptual and methodological reasons, belief in miracles can never be justified. In this chapter I will examine and assess these arguments.

Before commenting upon these arguments in detail, I think it is important to mention very briefly an assumption which underlies both Hume's thinking on miracles and most modern objections to them. It is the assumption that explanation and prediction are logically equivalent; that to be able to explain an event is to be able to predict it. The reader will recognize that I do not share this assumption. Part of my strategy for dealing with it has already emerged in chapters two and three. It will further emerge in the course of this and later chapters. For the moment, I wish only to stress that anyone who wants to defend belief in miracles can scarcely grant this assumption. Almost by definition, miracles are non-regular, unpredictable events. The believer must, therefore, argue that explanation is fundamentally explanation in terms of intelligibility, or of insight into the nature of reality, and only derivatively in terms of prediction capacity, since this will enable him to deny that any genuine explanation must also function as a prediction. This implies, of course, that even in the case of fairly straightforward scientific explanations, there is considerably more to be said than the brief sketch I gave at the beginning of chapter two indicated.

I think this is correct, but unnecessary for the point I wish to argue here. All I want to say is that, in my view, any appeal to the explanatory power of the laws of nature presupposes an appeal to a theory which is taken to provide insight into the nature of things. Prediction is valued, I suggest, not primarily because we want to manipulate nature, but because it is taken as an indication, but not a guarantee, that a theory which enables us to predict successfully provides genuine insight into the workings of nature.

McKINNON, MIRACLES, AND THE NATURAL COURSE OF EVENTS

One of the most forceful and ambitious objections to belief in miracles has been put forward by Alastair McKinnon in his famous article "Miracle and Paradox." In it, he argues that the term *miracle* "cannot consistently name or describe any real or alleged event."[1]

He begins by making two claims. The first is that "the concept of natural law, ... if it is to be allowed at all, is and must be universal in its application."[2] The second is that a miracle must be conceived as either: (1) "an event involving the suspension of natural law," or (2) "an event conflicting with our understanding of nature."[3] He then argues that each of these senses of miracle involves a contradiction and that the concept of miracle is therefore incoherent.

The problem with the first sense is that if we accept that the laws of nature "are simply highly generalized shorthand descriptions of how things do in fact happen"[4] then a miracle must be defined as an exception to what actually happened. As McKinnon puts it, a miracle would then be defined as "an event involving the suspension of the actual course of events." And someone who insisted upon describing an event as a miracle would be in the rather odd position of claiming that its occurrence was contrary to the actual course of events.[5]

Unfortunately, accepting the second sense of miracle also involves a contradiction. McKinnon claims it involves a contradiction in that,

[one] cannot believe both that the event happened and that the conception of nature with which it conflicts is adequate. In attempting to do so [one] necessarily contradicts [one]self. [One] is like the man who says "Yes this cat is white" then blandly adds "... but I hold that all cats are black."[6]

As he comments, "such a person may reasonably be asked to surrender either the historicity of the event or the conception of nature with which it conflicts."[7]

Of course, neither of these alternatives is acceptable in that neither makes it possible for the term *miracle* to describe any real or alleged event. On the one hand, to surrender historicity is to admit the term has no place in describing events in the real world. On the other hand, to revise our conception of nature is to repudiate the grounds upon which it was originally urged that the event was a miracle. We seem forced to conclude that the idea of a miracle is incoherent and hence a mere pseudo-concept.

Impressive though it seems, this argument is unsound. Both McKinnon's understanding of what it means for something to be a law of nature and his understanding of what it means for an event to be a miracle are incorrect. First, his claim that we may substitute the expression "the actual course of events" for the expression "natural law" seems simply false. Inasmuch as they are merely conditional statements, scientific laws cannot, by themselves, serve to predict or explain events. We cannot predict an event solely on the basis of the laws of nature, we must also know the relevant initial conditions to which the laws apply.[8] The terms *actual course of events* and *natural law* are not interchangeable.

Second, he is wrong to claim that a miracle must be conceived as either an event involving the suspension of the laws of nature or an event conflicting with our understanding of nature. As I have shown, a miracle need not be taken as indicating that the laws of nature no longer apply or are temporarily suspended. Rather it points to the fact that God, or possibly some other transcendent agent, has changed the material conditions to which the laws apply and so introduced into nature an event which nature would not otherwise have produced.

The essential difficulty with McKinnon's argument is that, having noted that a miracle is an event that is contrary to the natural course of events (an event which nature would not have produced on its own), he interprets this to mean that a miracle must be conceived as an event contrary to the actual course of events. Unless he is prepared to argue that it is inconceivable that an event could have a non-physical, non-natural cause, this conclusion is illegitimate. A miracle is contrary to the natural course of events not in the sense that it is an event which cannot actually happen, but in the sense that it cannot happen except through the action of an agent who transcends nature. If we grant that such events are at least logically conceivable, it appears, contra McKinnon, that the term *miracle* could consistently name or describe a real or allegedly real event.

NOWELL-SMITH AND PREDICTIVE EXPANSION

Another challenge to the legitimacy of the concept of a miracle has been put forward by Patrick Nowell-Smith, in his article "Miracles – The Philosophical Approach." He begins by noting that to call an event a miracle is to offer not just a description of the event, but also an explanation of its occurrence, since to call it a miracle is to engage not only in observation, but also in interpretation. Given that "evidence must be kept distinct from explanatory theory,"[9] even the best evidence can establish only that certain extraordinary phenomena sometimes occur. Having established the occurrence of an extraordinary event, it will not do automatically to call it a miracle. The question of whether extraordinary phenomena occur must be kept distinct from the question of whether these phenomena are properly called miracles.

The next step in his argument is to observe that "science is committed, not to definite theories or concepts, but to a certain method of explanation."[10] This means that, even though it might involve new terms and unfamiliar concepts, it might be possible at some future time to frame a strictly scientific explanation of the extraordinary events we are tempted to call miracles. Thus, "the problem is not whether science can explain everything in current terms but whether the explanation of 'miracles' requires a method quite different from that of science."[11]

Finally, he comments that a genuine explanation must always have predictive power and involve "a law or hypothesis capable of predictive expansion."[12] Further, in explaining a miracle, it makes no sense to make reference to presumed "supernatural" laws, since it is impossible to distinguish a "supernatural" law from a "natural" law. This leads to the conclusion that an event is either scientifically explicable or no explanation at all is possible: "the supernatural seems to dissolve on the one hand into the natural and on the other into the inexplicable."[13]

The chief problem with this argument is that it assumes the very thing it needs to demonstrate. The premise that a true explanation must always have predictive power and involve "a law or hypothesis capable of predictive expansion" is crucial to its success. This is a questionable claim, however. Scientific explanation does indeed involve citing a law or hypothesis capable of predictive expansion, but it is far from clear that scientific explanation is the only legitimate type of explanation.

In this regard, it is noteworthy that one of the necessary conditions for an event being a miracle is that it be brought about by a rational agent who in some way transcends nature. It is therefore significant that we distinguish between explanations which involve the purposes or intentions of agents and explanations which do not. *Prima facie,* these two types of explanation are radically different.[14]

In a scientific explanation an event E is the consequence of a certain set of relevant initial conditions and a certain set of relevant general laws. However, in what is sometimes termed a "personal" explanation[15] an event E is explained by reference to an agent's intention or purpose to accomplish E or a further event F. Further, this type of explanation differs from scientific explanation in that it need have no close connection to the notion of prediction and yet may still serve as an adequate explanation of an event. As Swinburne comments, "You could not discover my purpose and therefore my consequent action in going out the door now by noting what I always or normally did before going out the door."[16] Usually, if we wish to explain the actions of an agent, we must make reference to the agent's public utterances concerning his intentions and purposes. There is no parallel to this requirement in the case of scientific explanation.

Lest these brief remarks concerning explanation be miscontrued, I wish to emphasize that it is a controversial issue whether explanations involving references to the purposes of agents can be reduced to scientific explanations. One of the major tasks of those who believe in the occurrence of miracles must be to make clear the notion of agent causality and elaborate a world-view in which it acquires credibility. This is a large and complex task which I shall address in chapter six. For now, I only wish to emphasize that, *prima facie* at least, we must distinguish between two different types of explanation. One of these, it is true, always involves a law or hypothesis capable of predictive expansion, but the other does not. In light of the trend in recent philosophy to defend the legitimacy and importance of teleological explanations, it will not do for the critic of miracles simply to assume there is only one legitimate type of explanation.

CHRYSSIDES AND THE REPEATABILITY REQUIREMENT

As I have just indicated, the claim that explanations in terms of the purposes of agents need not be closely tied to the idea of predictive expansion is a controversial one. In an article entitled "Miracles and Agents," George Chryssides has argued that "the assignment of agency implies predictablity ... [and] no event can be assigned to an agent unless it is in principle possible to subsume the putative effect brought about by his action under scientific law."[17]

Underlying this comment is the problem of what distinguishes miracles from fortuitous coincidences. Chryssides provides us with the following hypothetical case to ponder.

Suppose Jones sees a mountain in the distance and says to the mountain, "Mountain, cast yourself into the sea!", whereupon the mountain is observed to rise up from its surroundings and fall into the water. If such a phenomenon occurred, why should we say that Jones moved the mountain, rather than Jones addressed the mountain in a certain way and that by a strange coincidence the mountain happened to move an instant later and fall into the water?[18]

He suggests that the answer we must give to this question is that miracles are distinguished from coincidences by virtue of the fact that calling an event a miracle implies, among other things, that it was caused by an agent. He also suggests that any claim that A caused B implies that B is in general repeatable on the occurrence of A and that this is a necessary condition of attributing causality. He calls this the Repeatability Requirement.[19]

He feels there is a problem in invoking the Repeatability Requirement, however. On the one hand, the believer must satisfy the Repeatability Requirement if she wishes to distinguish miracles from mere coincidences. On the other hand, if the believer satisfies the Repeatability Requirement she will be in a position to predict under what circumstances miracles occur and thus able to formulate some kind of law by which they can be predicted. In Chryssides' words:

Because the Repeatability Requirement must be satisfied in order to ascribe agency, either an allegedly miraculous event is a violation of scientific law, in which case it could not be performed by an agent, or else it is performed by an agent, in which case it could not be a violation of scientific law ... [I]n short ... there is an inherent self-contradiction in the notion of an agent performing a miracle.[20]

Impressive as it seems, this argument is seriously flawed. Several comments are in order. First, it should be emphasized that repeatability is not the sole criterion of rational agency. In many instances we attribute agency on the basis of context and intelligibility. Second, Chryssides errs in maintaining that those who believe in miracles cannot accept the Repeatability Requirement. He freely admits that

the Repeatability Requirement does not imply that we can state at what point in time any event attributed to a rational agent will recur ... To assign agency ... we do not need to be able to predict at what point in time the event will next recur; to assign agency (or to assign a cause) to an event is to imply that there is a likelihood of its recurring when certain relevant antecedent conditions are repeated. [21]

Put this way, however, the Repeatability Requirement is scarcely liable to prove a problem to those who believe in miracles. They will agree that miracles recur when certain relevant antecedent conditions are repeated. They will insist, though, that we take into consideration God's will as a relevant antecedent condition. Thus, they will maintain, "when God desires to perform other miracles, then like supernatural event follows from like supernatural cause (God)." [22] Finally, Chryssides too quickly assumes that if a miracle is a non-regular event which nature would not produce on its own then it must violate the laws of nature. This leads him to assume that if an agent produces an event which accords with the laws of nature it cannot be a miracle. However, as we saw in chapter two, this is a questionable assumption. With the possible exception of the Principle of the Conservation of Energy, there is no reason to think that a miracle violates any of the laws of nature.

ROBINSON AND THE PROBLEM OF CRITERIA

McKinnon, Nowell-Smith, and Chryssides have all taken the very strong view that the idea of a miracle is a pseudo-concept. Others, realizing that the idea is no mere pseudo-concept, have nevertheless argued that belief in the occurrence of miracles could never be justified. Their grounds for saying this are not that miracles are a logical impossibility, but that to call something a miracle would impose arbitrary limits on what is scientifically explicable. In developing this view, one of its most capable exponents, Guy Robinson, writes:

notice what would happen to the scientist if he allowed himself
to employ the concept of an irregularity in nature or of a miracle
in relation to his work. He would be finished as a scientist ... To
do this would be simply to resign, to opt out, as a scientist ...
Scientific development would either be stopped or else made
completely capricious, because it would necessarily be a matter
of whim whether one invoked the concept of miracle or irregularity to explain an awkward result, or on the other hand accepted
the result as evidence of the need to modify the theory one was
investigating. [23]

In essence, this is an objection that, because there exist no
criteria by which we may detemine whether "anomalies"
are properly regarded as miracles or as events that indicate
an inadequate understanding of natural processes, it is
impossible to justify the use of the term *miracle*. To invoke
the term, Robinson objects, is to set artificial and arbitrary
limits on scientific explanation.

In response to this argument it may be agreed that not
every way of postulating a miracle deserves consideration
and that a superstitious mentality in which they proliferate
must be avoided. However, I question whether it is impossible to develop criteria which would distinguish events
properly called miracles from events which properly
understood simply indicate an inadequate understanding of
natural processes.

Suppose the following criteria are met:
1 There is strong evidence that the event actually
   occurred.
2 The event took place in a context in which it can be
   seen to have moral and religious significance. [24]
3 Although it is carefully scrutinized, the event cannot
   be identified as being of some repeatable type. (It need
   not be unique, but merely of such a nature that it is not
   consistently repeatable.)
4 The regularity to which the event constitutes an excep-

tion is strongly confirmed and is known to apply to the same type of physical circumstances in which it happened.

I think these criteria serve to differentiate events which can legitimately be interpreted as miracles and events which are best interpreted as indices of an inadequate understanding of natural processes. It will not always be easy to apply them. There may well exist cases where it is no simple matter to decide whether these criteria have been met; it may prove difficult to decide whether the event can properly be seen as religiously significant, for instance. It has been well said, however, that the fact that twilight exists should not persuade us that day cannot be distinguished from night. The fact that cases may occur where we find it hard to decide whether the criteria apply does not detract from the fact that these criteria provide a non-arbitrary basis upon which to decide whether a particular event is best described as an anomaly or a miracle. I conclude, therefore, that whether we view an extraordinary event as a miracle or as the result of some unknown natural process need not be a matter of whim.

A possible response to this line of argument is that, although it may not be a matter of caprice or whim whether we call an event a miracle, miracle claims, no less than scientific claims, are corrigible. To call an event a miracle, therefore, is to hold that it is explained and to rule out the possiblity of any future scientific explanation of it. This objection, too, seems misguided. Two of the criteria for an event being considered a miracle are that it cannot be identified as being some repeatable type and that the regularity of nature to which it constitutes an exception is strongly confirmed and known to apply to the type of physical circumstances in which it happened. Clearly, there could be new scientific evidence which would suggest either that the event can be identified as being of some repeatable type or that the regularity of nature to which it constitutes an exception is not as strongly established as was previously thought. We would not, therefore, in terming it a "miracle," prematurely rule out the possibility of a future scientific explanation.

There is a related objection based on the fact that miracle claims are corrigible. It may be expressed as the claim that it is always more rational to believe that an event can be explained naturalistically if only we acquire the requisite scientific knowledge, than to believe that a miracle has occurred. The answer to this objection is found in the distinction which needs to be drawn between pragmatic working assumptions and metaphysical presuppositions. We may employ the principle of first seeking a natural explanation of an event without thereby committing ourselves to the position that a supernatural explanation of an event can never be legitimately postulated. N.L. Geisler is correct when he writes:

Simply to assume ... that there must be a naturalistic explanation for every event begs the question in favour of naturalism ... [A]doping the working procedure of always looking for a natural explanation need not be extended into a rigid naturalistic position that there are no nonnatural explanations. The scientific mind should not legislate what kind of explanations there can be.[25]

The theist, then, *may* employ the methodological principle of first looking for a natural explanation. However, I see no reason to insist that in all cases she *must* employ this principle, on pain of being irrational. Faced with an event like the Resurrection, it seems entirely rational to take as one's working assumption that it is a miracle. What is essential for rationality is not what initial interpretation is given, but that it be open to revision in the light of further information.

David Basinger seems to have missed this point when he criticizes Grace Jantzen for claiming that an event must be perceived as scientifically inexplicable before the theist will consider it miraculous.[26] He gives as a counter-example the case of a believer who, in the midst of a tornado alert, prays for safety and subsequently her house is the only one in the area which is not completely destroyed. He correctly notes that the believer may well interpret the event as a miracle. He also correctly notes that it is not obvious that such an event constitutes any overriding of nature by God. He draws from this the moral that a miracle need not be scientifically inexplicable, that is, an event produced by God overriding the usual course of nature. This seems wrong, however. It is exactly the believer's view that her house would not have been preserved had God not intervened and changed the course of nature. We may not think that her view is correct, but there can be no doubt that if she is right then the event is scientifically inexplicable. Like Holland in chapter one, Basinger's claim that examples of this sort demonstrate that an occurrence need not be perceived as scientifically inexplicable before the theist will consider it miraculous misses the point. It is precisely because she believes that God directly intervened to prevent what would have otherwise happened – and by doing this producing a scientifically inexplicable event – that the believer is persuaded that the preservation of her house is a miracle. It is possible to be mistaken about whether one of the necessary conditions for an event being a miracle has really been met, but this scarcely implies that the condition is not really necessary.

Put somewhat differently, my point is that the fact that miracle claims are corrigible does not imply that we are wrong to define miracles as events incapable of being given a naturalistic explanation. Neither does it imply that the believer must always initially assume that an event has a naturalistic explanation. Of course, there always remains the logical possibility that a revision of scientific law may lead to a naturalistic explanation of what was hitherto considered a miracle. This, however, can hardly be taken to justify the conclusion that it is always the more rational course to believe that all events have natural explanations. For example, given the fact that all scientific claims are corrigible, there is always the logical possibility that we are wrong in supposing that, in the normal course of events, the blood circulates in a living human body. It will not do, though, merely on the grounds that this claim is corrigible, to hold that some other alternative, such as the claim that we are mistaken in believing the blood to circulate, is equally probable or as well-established.[27]

It is theoretically possible that some revision of scientific law might enable us to offer a natural explanation of events we call miracles, but it is also true that it is possible that no revision would enable us to do this. Our decision as to which of these hypotheses is most probably true must be based on an assessment of how well they "fit" the evidence. Both alternatives may be logically possible but they are not necessarily equally probable. Thus Jantzen is quite correct when she maintains that "just as there could come a point where it would be irrational to deny that the event [i.e. the purported miracle] occurred, so there could at least in principle come a point beyond which it would be foolish to deny that it was genuinely miraculous."[28]

By way of illustrating this point more vividly, let us conduct a thought experiment. Suppose we hear of a man who claims to perform miracles of healing through the power of God. Upon investigating, we learn that this person has not only an exemplary character, but also the ability to perform remarkable cures. We are able to document occasions when, immediately following the prayers of this man, limbs lost to disease or accident were whole again within a matter of minutes, eyes severely damaged were restored to sight, and supposedly terminal diseases were reversed. Further, we find not only that he appears to have the power to heal any kind of disease or injury, but also that no interposition of lead screens or strong electromagnetic fields or the like has any observable effect on his ability to heal. Indeed, we observe that his power is apparently independent of distance, since people in distant countries have experienced dramatic healing after he prayed for their cure.

Such an example raises at least two problems for the person who holds that it is always more reasonable to postulate a natural explanation rather than accept the occurrence of a miracle. The first is that this procedure leads to an apparently unwarranted scepticism concerning our knowledge of the laws of nature. If we had good reason to accept that such extraordinary events occurred, and if we insisted that all physical events must be explained naturalistically, then we would have to be prepared to reject or revise the laws which led us to expect different results. This would place us in the position of questioning what were hitherto thought to be basic, well-evidenced, and accurate statements of the laws of nature. In short, we would be forced to adopt a position of radical scepticism concerning the claims of science. This, it must be noted, is in sharp contrast to the theist, who is able to offer an account of how we may accept the occurrence of such extraordinary events and yet retain faith in our knowledge of natural laws.

This is not to deny that science often progresses by rejecting previously accepted statements of natural law. To insist that phenomena such as those described in our hypothetical case would have to be interpreted naturalistically, no matter the context in which they occurred, is at least as great an act of faith as a religious interpretation of such events, however.

Indeed, it might require a greater act of faith to interpret such events naturalistically. The person who believes such events are miracles, taking her cue from Hume, might ask which is more likely: that a multitude of unknown processes which require us to revise or even reject well-established statements of the laws of nature fortuitously combined to produce an extraordinary and religiously significant event: or that an extraordinary and religiously significant event occurred which, although it does not force us to revise or reject any well-established statements of natural law, seems to indicate that a transcendent rational agent acted to produce in nature an event which nature would not have produced of itself. John Henry Newman, commenting on the "subtle question ... respecting the possible existence of causes in nature, to us unknown, by the supposed operation of which the apparent anomalies may be reconciled to the ordinary laws of the system,"[29] argued that,

it is impossible, from the nature of the case, absolutely to disprove any, even the wildest, hypothesis which may be framed ... It becomes, then, a balance of opposite probabilities, whether gratuitously to suppose a multitude of perfectly unknown causes, and these, moreover, meeting in one and the same history, or to have recourse to one, and that a known power, then miraculously exerted for an extraordinary and worthy object.[30]

Given this, only a dogmatic and uncritical metaphysical assumption that nature is immune to any influence by something other than itself can explain the insistence of some thinkers that, no matter what the event might be and no matter what the context in which it may occur, it would always be more rational to live in the faith that it has a natural explanation than to believe it to be a miracle.

The defender of naturalistic interpretation must overcome a second difficulty, for his claim that extraordinary phenomena must have a natural explanation tends to lose its meaning. In the case of our hypothetical example, what would it mean to call the power to heal "natural" if it were shown that this capacity was not affected by distance, by any kind of physical screening, or by the specific disease or injury of the person in need of healing? Could we legitimately use the word *natural* to describe a capacity that appears to be entirely independent of other natural forces and capacities? The naturalist cannot hold that naturalism is compatible with any logically possible state of affairs in the world without leaving himself vulnerable to the charge that he makes his view invulnerable by making it untestable and hence unfalsifiable.

Even in the hypothetical case described above, the naturalist might reply, it would be difficult to demonstrate that a certain ability is truly independent of physical limitations. The logical possibility that our miracle-worker is bounded by conditions as yet undiscovered would always remain. Thus, it could never be entirely clear that the healer's capacity to heal is not affected by distance or is truly independent of other natural forces and capacities.

This response evades rather than resolves the issue. To invoke it leaves the naturalist in the awkward position of justifying her rejection of evidence to the contrary. The fact that evidence concerning matters of fact can never be conclusive does not entail the conclusion that we must suspend judgment concerning their nature – otherwise science would be an impossibility. We must reach provisional conclusions on the basis of the evidence available, but they may be strongly established and, in the absence of contrary evidence, deserve our rational assent. Conceivably, as in the case of our hypothetical example, there could be instances where an abundance of evidence indicates the exercise of capacities which are independent of physical limitations.

The claim, therefore, that we must always postulate a natural explanation of an event, however improbable that explanation may be, is at best false, at worst meaningless. At best it begs the question of whether nature may be considered an isolated system suffering no intrusions from something other than itself. At worst, it is vulnerable to the charge that it is explanatorily impotent by virtue of the fact that it proves compatible with any conceivable state of affairs or series of events in the world.

CHAPTER FIVE

Physicalism and the Conservation of Energy

In chapter two I discussed the relation between miracles and the laws of nature. I argued that, with the possible exception of the Principle of the Conservation of Energy, miracles need not be conceived as violations of the laws of nature. I argued that we must distinguish between what I called the weak form of the Principle, namely the claim that energy is conserved in a causally isolated system, and its strong form, namely the claim that energy can neither be created nor destroyed. Miracles, I argued, are consistent with the truth of the weak form of the Principle, but not with its strong form. I further noted that it is the weak form that is directly supported by the experimental evidence and that if we wish to arrive at the strong form a further inference is required.

In this chapter, I will argue that there is a good reason to think that the weak form of the Principle is a law of nature, but that the strong form is not. I will argue that the strong form functions as a defining-postulate of physicalism[1] and cannot be confirmed on the basis of evidence which confirms belief in the weak form. To object to miracles on the basis of the strong form is, therefore, merely to assume the truth of physicalism and to beg the question of whether miracles occur.

EVIDENCE AND THE TWO FORMS OF
THE PRINCIPLE OF THE CONSERVATION OF ENERGY

Earlier, in chapter three, we saw that Hume's "balance-of-probabilities" argument has serious flaws and that if it is to have any force at all against belief in miracles it must be demonstrated that the strong form of the Principle of the Conservation of Energy is a well-evidenced law of nature. In this form, the Principle functions as a defining-postulate of physicalism; it is something that must be true if the physical universe is to be conceived as being wholly independent and self-contained. Its truth, therefore, cannot be merely assumed. By definition, miracles are events produced by an agent who transcends nature, so it is small wonder that reports of them cannot be considered credible if we begin by presupposing the truth of physicalism.

The question is how the advocate of Hume's argument – now revealed to be a physicalist – is to demonstrate the truth of the strong form. His most plausible course of action seems to be to argue that the experimental evidence which confirms belief in the weak form of the Principle also confirms belief in its strong form. Thus he may claim that to the degree that belief in the weak form is justified so belief in the strong form is justified.

The physicalist who attempts to argue in this manner is, I think, mistaken. He cannot simply appeal to the large body of experimental evidence which supports the conclusion that in a causally isolated system energy remains constant. As we saw in chapter two, this evidence is entirely consistent with the possible occurrence of miracles. To say that energy is conserved in an isolated system is not to address the question of whether the physical universe is isolated in the sense that it is not influenced by the action of some transcendent agent. To say that miracles occur is not to deny that in a causally isolated system energy is conserved. Belief in miracles, therefore, does not force us to deny any of the evidence usually cited as confirming belief in the Principle of the Conservation of Energy.

True, the claim that energy is conserved in a causally isolated system is consistent with the claim that energy can neither be created nor destroyed, but it does not imply this claim, and the evidence which supports it does not warrant drawing the far stronger conclusion that energy can neither be created nor destroyed. What this means is that the body of evidence supporting the claim that in a causally isolated system energy will be conserved is neutral as regards the further question of whether or not there exists something capable of creating or destroying energy, since it implies nothing concerning the further question of whether or not the physical universe is in fact causally isolated in the relevant sense of not being subject to the will of a transcendent agent.

The physicalist may protest that I have ignored what is known in confirmation theory as the converse consequence condition. This condition states that if a body of evidence e, confirms a hypothesis h_1, and if there exists another hypothesis h_2, which implies h_1, then e also confirms h_2. For example, "those experimental findings which confirm Galileo's law, or Kepler's laws are considered also as confirming Newton's law of gravitation."[2] Thus, in the present instance, the physicalist may argue that, since the weak form of the Principle of the Conservation of Energy can be deduced from its strong form, the empirical evidence which confirms belief in the weak form of the Principle also confirms belief in its strong form.

In response, it must be pointed out that the converse consequence condition is not generally satisfiable and cannot be accepted as a general rule of the logic of confirmation. Consider the following counterexample: for any a and c put $b \equiv a \vee c$. Then $a \rightarrow b$, and by the entailment condition (that is, if $a \rightarrow b$ then a confirms b), a confirms b. Hence by the converse consequence condition a confirms c, since c

entails *b*. It is impossible, on pain of everything confirming everything, that a non-trivial relation of confirmation subsist between every pair of statements and thus if entailment is retained the converse consequence condition must be rejected.[3]

To be fair, it must be admitted that often a body of data which confirms a particular hypothesis *h* is considered also to confirm a stronger hypothesis from which *h* may be deduced. The example cited earlier holds true: we regard the body of data which confirms Galileo's and Kepler's laws as also confirming Newton's law of gravitation and feel that we are justified in so doing. However, as Carl Hempel observes, such examples do not justify accepting the converse consequence condition as a general rule, for in such examples the weaker hypothesis is invariably connected with the stronger one by a logical bond of a particular kind. In such instances, the weaker hypothesis is essentially a substitution instance of the stronger hypothesis.[4] Thus, although neither Galileo in developing his terrestrial physics nor Kepler in developing his celestial physics talked of forces, their laws, in the clear vision of hindsight, can be seen to be approximations to Newton's general law of gravitation which refers to the force between any two bodies. Even if as approximations these laws need some revision and correction in the light of Newton's law, they are viewed as being essentially instances of his more general law of gravitation. In instances where this special logical relation exists, it does seem reasonable to view the evidence as confirming both hypotheses, for the stronger hypothesis is, essentially, just a more general form of the weaker more specific hypothesis and does not contain any extraneous elements which the evidence does not confirm.

The physicalist, noting that strictly speaking the laws of Galileo and Kepler are not mere substitution instances of the laws of Newton, might be tempted to argue that the relation between the strong and the weak forms of the Principle is analogous and that the application of the converse consequence principle is therefore legitimate. However, it must be emphasized that in cases where the converse consequence condition is legitimately applied it is always possible to bring some additional independent evidence which helps confirm the stronger hypothesis and ensures that any additional elements introduced by it are not gratuitous. Thus Newton did not offer his hypothesis simply as an explanation of the laws of Galileo and Kepler, but could claim additional support. In the case of the strong form of the Principle this cannot be done, since there exists no additional body of evidence which would tend to confirm the otherwise gratuitous view that energy can neither be created nor destroyed. The two cases are not, therefore, analogous.

The problem the physicalist faces is that in cases such as the strong and the weak forms of the Principle where this special relation does not exist (where the stronger hypothesis is not just a more general form of the weaker hypothesis), and where there exists no independent evidence in favour of the stronger hypothesis, the converse consequence condition becomes "entirely absurd."[5] The strong form of the Principle, although it implies the weaker hypothesis that energy is conserved in a causally isolated system, contains the further assumption that energy is uncreated and indestructible. It is clear this assumption need not be confirmed by the evidence which confirms the weaker hypothesis that energy is conserved in a causally isolated system. Thus the evidence which confirms belief in the weak form of the Principle cannot be taken to confirm belief in its strong form. The physicalist cannot appeal to the converse consequence condition. The body of evidence which supports belief in the weak form of the Principle is neutral as regards the further question of whether energy may be created or destroyed.

Faced with this, the most promising course of action for the physicalist seems to be to revise the converse consequence principle somewhat and argue that if e (e.g., a body of experimental evidence),confirms h_1 (e.g., the weak form of the Principle), and h_2 (e.g., the strong form of the Principle), explains h_1 then e confirms h_2. His strategy will be to argue that the weak form of the Principle is a lower-level law which needs to be explained on the basis of some deep structural assumption. The strong form of the Principle, with its deep structural assumption that energy can be neither created nor destroyed, provides an explanation of the weak form and hence all the inductive support of the weak form can be regarded as "flowing upward" so as to support the strong form of the Principle.

Without denying the legitimacy of demanding an explanation of the weak form of the Principle, I want to stress that the physicalist is on shaky ground if he attempts to argue in this manner. The history of science is replete with deep structural assumptions which were made in order to explain certain lower-level laws, but which were later abandoned. Theories of the aether, of phlogiston, and of spontaneous generation, to name only a few, have all, at one time or another, been proposed as deep structural assumptions necessary to explain well-evidenced lower-level laws.

Lest the physicalist be tempted to reply that there are good deep structural assumptions and bad deep structural assumptions, and that the strong form of the Principle constitutes a good deep structural assumption, I wish to draw an important distinction. At this point in the discussion what is at issue is whether the belief that energy can neither be created nor destroyed is confirmed, not whether it is a belief which is plausible. I am not arguing that belief in the strong form of the Principle is implausible – that is a further question which I shall address later in this chapter and in chapter six – only that it is unconfirmed. This distinction is a necessary one. A belief may be plausible even though it is not confirmed. To say that a belief is plausible is to say that it is a reasonable belief to hold on the basis of available evidence; to say that a belief is confirmed is to say that the evidence in some way guarantees that the belief is true. To claim that a belief is plausible is not to deny the very real possibility that as more evidence becomes available this belief must be discarded because the additional evidence disconfirms it, but to claim that a belief is confirmed is to deny that there is further evidence which will disconfirm it.

The physicalist is likely to respond that it is impossible to talk of evidence "guaranteeing" belief. Surely all beliefs concerning matters of fact are corrigible. Surely it is conceivable that even the best confirmed scientific beliefs might be false. What then does this distinction amount to?

It amounts to this. Without denying that even the best-confirmed beliefs are corrigible, we must nevertheless distinguish between beliefs which we have reason to think will never be disconfirmed and beliefs about which we must suspend judgment concerning whether they will be disconfirmed. Those beliefs which we have good reason to think will never be disconfirmed we regard as confirmed, those about which we must suspend judgment we regard as plausible, but not confirmed.

It is the various ways in which evidence may be linked to belief which permits us to draw this distinction. In the case of a confirmed belief a wide variety of evidence is linked to that belief in a number of different ways by a number of independent hypotheses. In other words, we have a network of converging hypotheses, each of which finds it necessary to postulate the truth of that belief. It is this convergence which provides us with good reason to think that the belief is actually true. Of course it is not logically impossible that the belief might be false, but this convergence gives good reason to believe that this is not in fact the case. For example, although it is conceivable that the claim that the blood circulates in a normal living human body might be false, the wide variety of evidence and the large number of independent hypotheses which support this claim make its falsity very improbable.

In the case of a belief which is plausible, but not confirmed, we find neither such a wide variety of evidence nor the evidence linked to the belief in a number of different ways by a number of independent hypotheses. In such a case, the connection between evidence and belief is more like a chain than a network. It is this which teaches us that, although the belief may be plausible, it is nevertheless unconfirmed. The belief may be an attractive one, but, in the absence of a wide variety of evidence and a convergence of independent hypotheses, it remains only a possible interpretation of the evidence thought to support it.[6]

To revert to our examples of aether, phlogiston, and spontaneous generation, these are all cases of beliefs which, at the time they were proposed, were plausible beliefs. They provided explanations of the lower-level laws they were invoked to explain and were consistent with the available evidence. Nevertheless, it would be a mistake to think that these beliefs were confirmed, a mistake made amply clear by the subsequent course of science.

I wish to emphasize that my point is not that explanations of lower-level laws should not be sought; nor is it that deep structural explanations are illegitimate. Rather, it is that we cannot automatically conclude that the evidence which supports lower-level laws confirms the deep structural assumptions thought to be necessary to explain them. The problem in assuming that the evidence which confirms a lower-level law also confirms our deep structural assumption is that it may be possible to offer some other deep structural assumption which equally well explains the lower-level law. Thus, the problem in assuming that the evidence which confirms belief in the weak form of the Principle also confirms belief in the strong form is that it may be possible to offer some deep structural assumption other than the assumption that energy can neither be created nor destroyed, which can equally well explain the weak form of the Principle.

The physicalist is quite correct to demand an explanation of the truth of the weak form of the Principle. She is also on firm ground in proposing a hypothesis which explains the weak form of the Principle – her hypothesis that energy can neither be created nor destroyed. She errs, however, if she thinks the evidence for the weak form of the Principle also confirms its strong form. It is true that the hypothesis that energy can neither be created nor destroyed is consistent with the experimental results confirming belief in the weak form of the Principle . It may even be that, in the absence of a rival hypothesis capable of explaining the weak form, we are justified in accepting it as the best explanation of the weak form of the Principle. Nevertheless, the experimental evidence which confirms belief in the weak form of the Principle does not confirm belief in its strong form. Unless the physicalist can point to some independent body of evidence, the connection between the strong form of the Principle and the empirical evidence which supports belief in the weak form of the Principle remains very tenuous. In other words, unless the physicalist can demonstrate that the relation between the empirical evidence and her deep structural assumption is that of a network of converging hypotheses and not a fragile chain, she has no right to talk of confirmation of the strong form of the Principle. The experimental evidence which supports belief in the weak form of the Principle no more confirms the belief that energy can neither be created nor destroyed than the results of seventeenth, eighteenth, and nineteenth century physics confirm the existence of aether. The problem the physicalist faces is that there does not exist, and cannot exist, an additional body of empirical evidence to which she can appeal. The most she can ever show by measuring quantities of energy is that it is conserved in a causally isolated system. This, however, only confirms the weak, not the strong, form of the Principle. It is therefore impossible, even in principle, for her to confirm her deep structural claim that energy can neither be created nor destroyed. Note that I am not suggesting that in general it is impossible to confirm deep structural claims, only that this particular deep structural claim could never be confirmed.

It is important to realize that this does not mean that the strong form of the Principle cannot be disconfirmed. Additional evidence may serve to disconfirm a deep structural assumption, yet leave untouched the lower-level law the deep structural assumption was invoked to explain. For example, Pasteur was able to offer some new evidence and an alternative explanation of why maggots often appear in dead meat. He was thus able to dispense with the deep structural assumption of spontaneous generation. In the present case, the occurrence of miracles would serve to disconfirm the strong form of the Principle. Miracles, as I have observed, are consistent with the weak form of the Principle, but are inconsistent with the strong form, inasmuch as they imply that energy may be created or destroyed.

Thus we have been led to an interesting conclusion. It is that the strong form of the Principle cannot ever be confirmed, but that it could conceivably be disconfirmed. Confirming evidence cannot "flow upward" so as to confirm it, but additional evidence – for example, the occurrence of a miracle – might serve to disconfirm it. In so doing it would leave untouched the weak form of the Principle.

Pictured, the situation looks something like the diagram opposite.

We have seen that the physicalist cannot argue that the evidence which confirms belief in the weak form of the Principle also confirms belief in the strong form of the Principle. Given this, the question which arises is whether the physicalist, abandoning her attempt to argue that the evidence which confirms the weak form also confirms the strong form, is in a position to claim that belief in the strong form is nevertheless justified.

Evidence and the Principle of the Conservation of Energy

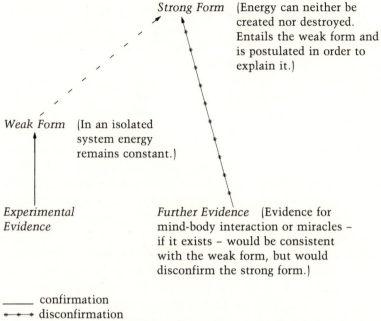

Strong Form   (Energy can neither be
created nor destroyed.
Entails the weak form and
is postulated in order to
explain it.)

Weak Form   (In an isolated
system energy
remains constant.)

Experimental
Evidence

Further Evidence   (Evidence for
mind-body interaction or miracles –
if it exists – would be consistent
with the weak form, but would
disconfirm the strong form.)

‾‾‾‾ confirmation
∗—∗—∗ disconfirmation
– – – consistent with but neither confirms nor disconfirms

There are two arguments by which she may attempt to
support such a view. First, she may attempt to argue that
the strong form is justified on the basis of Occam's Razor.
Thus, she may argue that there exists no positive evidence
that energy is ever created or destroyed. Given the basic
principle that we ought not to multiply entities needlessly,
we ought not then to postulate the existence of something
capable of creating or destroying energy. We are justified,
therefore, in concluding that energy can neither be created
nor destroyed.

Unfortunately for the physicalist, this is a very weak
argument. She is proposing that since there exists no

evidence that energy is ever created or destroyed we ought to accept the strong form of the Principle on the basis of Occam's Razor. The problem she faces is that the existence of such evidence is precisely what is at issue. The occurrence of miracles would constitute evidence that energy is sometimes created or destroyed. Faced with the reports of such events, it will not do to dismiss them on the grounds that miracles are antecedently improbable by virtue of the fact that they imply the falsity of the strong form of the Principle. The physicalist can point to no positive body of evidence in favour of the strong form and is thus in no position to frame a balance-of-probabilities argument designed to show that miracles are antecedently improbable by virtue of the fact that the evidence in their favour conflicts with a stronger body of evidence in favour of the strong form of the Principle.

Appealing to Occam's Razor, therefore, does not help the cause of the physicalist. On such an argument the sole justification for accepting the strong form of the Principle lies in a presumed lack of evidence that energy is ever created or destroyed. Faced with positive evidence that miracles occur, the physicalist is in no position to deny the likelihood of their occurrence.

Second, the physicalist may attempt to argue that, other than the hypothesis that energy can neither be created nor destroyed, there are no hypotheses capable of explaining the truth of the weak form of the Principle. Granted that this hypothesis is not confirmed by the evidence, it is nevertheless the only explanation available and we are justified in believing it. Should another hypothesis be put forward which better explains the weak form then the hypothesis that energy can neither be created nor destroyed must be abandoned, but in the absence of such an alternative hypothesis we are fully justified in believing that energy can neither be created nor destroyed. A variant of this argument would be for the physicalist to admit the existence of other hypotheses capable of explaining the weak form of the Principle, but to argue that her hypothesis is superior to any of its rivals.

I propose to deal more fully with the issue raised by this latter argument in my next chapter where I discuss the nature of world-views and whether they may be falsified. I think it fair to comment, however, that even if her argument is entirely successful the physicalist is in no position to frame a Humean type balance-of-probabilities argument designed to show there is a conflict between the evidence taken to support our belief in the Principle of the Conservation of Energy and the evidence in favour of miracles. It is clear that the evidence which supports belief in miracles conflicts not with any of the evidence which supports belief in the Principle of the Conservation of Energy, but with what the physicalist believes to be the best explanation of the fact that in a causally isolated system energy is conserved. Assuming her opponent can point to some positive body of evidence in favour of miracles, the physicalist has no grounds upon which she can dismiss such evidence. She can point to no evidence which confirms her view that energy can neither be created nor destroyed. It will not do, therefore, when faced with alleged instances of miracles, to argue that these events are antecedently improbable by virtue of the fact that they imply the falsity of the Principle of the Conservation of Energy.

CHAPTER SIX

World-Views and Falsification

The thrust of my last few chapters has been to argue that philosophical objections to miracles usually assume the very thing they need to prove. They implicitly assume that physicalism is true and that there exists only one legitimate type of explanation. On this account, the force they might otherwise have is largely vitiated.

However, it will scarcely do for the believer to leave the matter thus. To remove objections is not at all to establish grounds for belief. The physicalist can justifiably demand that the believer provide some positive grounds for belief in miracles. What this must amount to, eventually, is elaborating and defending a world-view other than physicalism. To claim that miracles occur is not just to hold that the strong form of the Principle of the Conservation of Energy, and hence physicalism, is false. To call an event a miracle is not merely to offer a description, but also an interpretation, of it. This presupposes the truth of some alternative world-view, namely theism, in which the concept of the miraculous can be embedded and seen to make sense. It is important, therefore, to say something about world-views in general and physicalism and theism in particular.

I want to explore three issues. First, I should like to consider an objection recently raised by Christine Overall against the claim that calling an event a miracle presupposes the truth of theism. She maintains that calling something a miracle presupposes not the truth, but the falsity, of theism. Second, I want to comment further on the issue of whether a world-view may be falsified. Earlier, I suggested there could conceivably exist evidence which would falsify physicalism. This is a claim that will not go unchallenged, however. Many philosophers hold that evidence is only evidence in the context of a theory in which it is seen to be significant and cannot, therefore, serve to disconfirm rival theories. Although I have already given some reasons for thinking that this view is mistaken, I want to say something more on the issue. Finally, I shall say something about what is involved in showing that theism is more probably true than physicalism.

MIRACLES AS COGNITIVE EVILS

In a recent article entitled "Miracles as Evidence against the Existence of God," Christine Overall claims that "there has been far too little attention paid to the alleged evidential connections between the existence of miracles and the existence of God."[1] She asserts that any event we might be prepared to call a miracle would not be evidence for, but against, the existence of God as traditionally conceived. Thus,

if a miracle ... were to occur, it in fact would constitute evidence against the existence of the Christian God. So, far from its being the case that identifying event x as a miracle would require one first to know that it is caused by God or a god, on the contrary, if one knew that God exists, then probably nothing could be identified as a miracle, and conversely, if event x could be identified as a miracle, one would have good reason to believe that God does not exist. Put simply my view is that a miracle ... is inconsistent with the concept of God.[2]

Her claim is interesting, but seems false. I would like to rehearse her argument before analysing it, since it has a shape and development that would be obscured if I were to intermingle exposition and criticism.

Overall begins by noting that the theist generally considers "the supposed order, regularity and harmony of the universe as evidence of the existence of a benign and omnipotent god."[3] Rejecting the view that to call an event a miracle is, by definition, to say that God exists, she goes on to urge that if the theist believes that the regularity and harmony of the universe constitute evidence for God's existence he can scarcely argue that miracles are also evidence for God's existence. She feels that, because they are irregular events, miracles must be thought of as "moment[s] of chaos ... gap[s] in the spatio-temporal structure"[4] of the universe. If God is conceived as a God of order and harmony, miracles do not constitute evidence for His existence, but rather His nonexistence.

Anticipating the reply that miracles reveal not meaningless gaps, but an intelligible pattern of divine activity, she attempts to demonstrate that miracles could never be consistent with God's supposed purposes and intentions. She argues that miracles would frustrate our attempts to gain knowledge of the world. She writes:

The extreme rarity of miracles, and the difficulties and controversies in identifying them, are an impediment to the growth of scientific and philosophical comprehension. A benevolent God would not mislead his people.[5]

She foresees two replies to this claim. The first is that miracles need not be considered mere dysteleological surds plaguing scientific accounts of the world, but rather parts of a pattern formed by divine intervention in the natural order. The second is that even if miracles wreak havoc with our understanding of the world, this is a small price to pay considering their positive benefits, the healing of a child or the revival of religious awareness, for example.

Commenting on the first of these replies, she claims that the rarity of miracles militates against any such response. She thinks this rarity has a twofold implication. If miracles occur infrequently then it will be difficult to discern any pattern of meaning in their occurrence, but if they occur frequently they will disrupt our efforts to see the world as forming a coherent, unified whole. She goes on to argue that the theist cannot admit the occurrence of miracles and still believe in the autonomy of science, "for by its very nature, any alleged 'pattern' of miraculous occurrences is inconsistent with the pattern of natural events which science seeks to account for."[6]

In response to the second of these replies, namely that in fulfilling the purposes of God the benefits of a miracle outweigh any epistemological difficulties it produces, she makes two comments. First, she claims that miracles are not an appropriate means for fulfilling God's purposes because "they ... seem to make use of human weaknesses – for example, fear, suggestibility, ignorance and awe of the unknown."[7] Second, and she considers this the more important criticism, "this appeal to God's purposes creates an opening for some of the same moves that are made in the argument from evil against God's existence."[8] She claims that if the divine purposes are to accomplish good, communicate divine teaching, or revive religious awareness miracles can scarcely be adequate to their accomplishment: "if we consider the standard Biblical examples of miracles, they reflect a certain caprice – one is cured, another is not; bias – in favour of one group of people over another; and triviality."[9] She adds that even if we do not use these events as standard examples of miracles "still the very fact that a miracle is an event, and therefore limited in space and time (albeit detached from the natural space-time continuum) means that it is inherently handicapped for conveying the purpose of a limitless God."[10]

Although she does not so characterize it, Overall's argument is basically a variation on the problem of evil. Miracles are seen as constituting a cognitive evil inasmuch as they prevent us from understanding the world, and a good God could not allow them to occur. Any evidence, therefore, for the existence of the Judaeo-Christian God is evidence against miracles and any evidence for miracles is evidence against the existence of such a God. Philosophers differ on how serious a challenge the existence of evil poses to theism. There is, however, no need to delve deeply into the problem of evil in order to rebut her argument. Whether or not it has any force depends on whether miracles really constitute cognitive evils. If they do not then her argument cannot even get started. What I propose to show is that she does not provide us with any good reasons for thinking miracles are a cognitive evil.

My first criticism is that Overall misdefines miracles. She considers a miracle to be either a violation of the laws of nature or a permanently inexplicable event. Neither definition is adequate. I have already shown that a miracle, in the strong sense of an event which nature would not produce on its own, can occur in a world which behaves completely in accordance with the laws of nature. In suggesting that a miracle can be defined as a permanently inexplicable event, Overall follows David Basinger. Unfortunately, Basinger seems confused on this point. He takes the phrase "permanently inexplicable" to be equivalent to the phrase "not subsumable under natural law."[11] This, however, is to beg the question of what form an explanation may take. Miracles are usually conceived to be, in some sense, direct acts of God. Both in Scripture and more modern accounts they are *explained* by referring to the desires and purposes of a transcendent agent. As I have already shown, what Swinburne has called "personal explanation," or explanation in terms of agency, is a concept essential to the notion of the miraculous and, provided it can be defended, there is no reason to define miracles as permanently inexplicable

events. Indeed, to attempt to do so is to betray a misunderstanding of how the term is actually used. Those who
believe in miracles do not think of them as permanently
inexplicable events, but rather as events which especially
reveal the character and purposes of God.

Overall might be tempted to reply that my criticisms of
her definitions miss the point entirely. She might argue that
precisely what is at issue is whether certain special and
unusual events can be linked to God. We cannot begin,
therefore, with a definition which assumes God's role in
producing the event.

Tempting though it might be, such a reply would not
prove successful. By way of seeing why, let me distinguish
two questions: (1) "What is a miracle?" and (2) "What
events are properly called miracles?" Note that the first
question concerns the intension of the term *miracle*,
whereas the second question concerns its extension. Note
also that extension is determined by intension, not the
other way around. [12] Put somewhat differently, my point is
that before we can answer the question "What events are
properly called miracles?" we must answer the question
"What is a miracle?" In her discussion, Overall seems to
have the problem backwards. She assumes that we can
readily identify miracles as a class and that our problem is
one of abstracting a definition so as to arrive at the meaning
of the term. She then proceeds to redefine the term, arriving
in the process at a definition that has little resemblance to
the way the word is actually used. [13] Given the definitions
she proposes, it is hardly surprising that miracles prove inconsistent with the existence of God. She leaves unexamined, however, the logically prior question of whether her
definitions have captured what we ordinarily mean by the
term *miracle*.

My second criticism is that she is wrong to hold that if
miracles occur they frustrate any attempt to understand the

world. To call an event a miracle *is* to explain it; it is to explain it in terms of God's purposes and desires. If a miracle occurs, and we recognize it to be such, we understand the world better. Only if we accept her redefinition of a miracle as a permanently inexplicable event does it follow necessarily that a miracle is an impediment to the growth of scientific and philosophical comprehension. As I remarked above, the problem is not in understanding what is meant by the term *miracle*, but in correctly applying it.

Neither will it do merely to assert that "by its very nature, any alleged 'pattern' of miraculous occurrences is inconsistent with the pattern of natural events which science seeks to account for ..."[14] The demand that all reality be interrelated and consistent is a legitimate one. However, to insist that any alleged pattern of miraculous occurrences cannot be consistent with the pattern of natural events is to beg the question of whether nature constitutes the whole of reality or is only a partial system within it – and thereby to beg the question of whether miracles are a cognitive evil. Unless we presuppose the falsity of theism, the epistemic dissonance Overall speaks of is more apparent than real. It seems quite possible for the theist to relate these two patterns. As C.S. Lewis notes:

In the forward direction (i.e. during the time which follows its occurrence) it [a miracle] is interlocked with all Nature just like any other event. Its peculiarity is that it is not in that way interlocked backwards, interlocked with the previous history of Nature ... [T]he miracle and the previous history of Nature may be interlocked ... but not in the way the Naturalist expected: rather in a much more roundabout fashion. The great complex event called Nature, and the new particular event introduced into it by the miracle, are related by their common origin in God, and doubtless, if we knew enough, most intricately related in His purpose and design, so that a Nature which had had a different history, and therefore been a different Nature, would have been invaded by different miracles or by none at all. In that way the miracle and the previous course of Nature are as well interlocked as any other two realities, but you must go back as far as their common Creator to find the interlocking. You will not find it within Nature ... Everything is connected with everything else: but not all things are connected by the short and straight roads we expected. [15]

Leaving aside her assertion that the standard Biblical examples of miracles reflect a certain caprice, bias, and triviality – it is hard to reply to this charge unless she is willing to argue more specifically [16] – I want to offer a final criticism of Overall's position. Towards the end of her argument she asserts that, because it is an event and therefore limited in space and time, a miracle is inherently inadequate for conveying the purposes of God. This is a very curious claim. How is God to convey His purposes to spatio-temporal creatures except through events of some sort? Does it not follow from the very fact that we are creatures bound by space and time that God cannot make known His purposes to a particular person at a particular place at a particular time except through a particular event or series of events? Certainly prayers no less than miracles presuppose a spatio-temporal setting. Unless she is prepared to argue that it is logically impossible that God can communicate with spatio-temporal creatures at all, Overall cannot claim that the mere fact that miracles are events limited in time and space entails that they are inadequate vehicles for conveying God's purposes. However, she gives no indication that she wants to claim this and, significantly, gives no argument capable of supporting such a view. Her claim that a miracle cannot convey the purposes of God remains unsupported, therefore, as does her claim that the occurrence of a miracle constitutes evidence against the existence of God.

WORLD-VIEWS AND FALSIFICATION

I wish now to say something further about the issue of whether world-views may be falsified. Put simply, a world-view constitutes a coherent, or at least apparently coherent, set of basic beliefs about the fundamental character of reality.[17] It provides its adherents with a framework or system of beliefs within which to theorize, and thus plays a large role in their treatment of specific philosophical issues. The problems that they are inclined to regard as genuine rather than spurious, the possible solutions they are inclined to investigate as being viable (as opposed to those they feel they are wasting their time and effort in investigating) all these are in a large and important part influenced by their commitment to a particular world-view. Of course, this is not to say that what a person committed to the truth of a particular world-view will say concerning a specific philosophical issue is completely determined. There may be, indeed there usually are, a number of possible views consistent with the truth of a particular world-view. However, it is clear that a world-view does set parameters within which those committed to its truth are constrained to theorize.[18]

World-views, because of their comprehensiveness, are very difficult to falsify. Many philosophers have noted that falsification becomes progressively more difficult as we move from the level of simple experimental laws and limited theories to the level of comprehensive theories and paradigms and finally to the level of metaphysical assumptions and world-views. Indeed some, having noted the fact that it seems impossible to specify in advance any "crucial experiment" which decides with finality between even low-level theories,[19] have concluded that world-views cannot be falsified. Evidence, they contend, is only evidence in the framework of some theory in which it is seen to be significant. It cannot, therefore, serve to overthrow a rival theory, since the rival theory will always either cease to regard it as significant data, and hence cease to regard it as evidence, or else reinterpret it and account for it in some other way. On this account, it is maintained, world-views such as physicalism and theism are impossible to falsify.

Although many thinkers, especially those concerned to defend religious beliefs, have endorsed this holistic view, it is nevertheless premature to think that world-views are impossible to falsify. It is certainly true that a world-view may always be "saved" by a certain amount of tinkering, but if this tinkering is purely *ad hoc* it is bound to appear unjustified and implausible. To conclude that world-views are immune to falsification because such tinkering is always possible is to miss the point that there is a sense in which we may speak of discordant data or counter-evidence, namely data which cannot be explained or reinterpreted within the confines of a world-view, except on the basis of purely *ad hoc* assumptions. If the amount of such tinkering required becomes too great then this counts as a legitimate reason for abandoning a world-view. [20]

Neither will it do to argue, as have some holists, that, since there are no privileged analytic truths connecting the language of evidence with the language of theory, there can be no empirical data which can serve as evidence for an alternative world-view, unless the truth of that world-view is already presupposed. It is quite right to think that there must exist links between the language of evidence and the language of theory if evidence is to be used to confirm theoretical claims. What is not required, however, is that these links consist of analytic truths. These links may be provided by the theory to be tested – in the case of miracles a theistic world-view – so long as they are not used in such a way as to guarantee that the theory will be positively instantiated whatever the evidence might be.

Of course it is necessary to take certain precautions in

evaluating evidence. It is important to test a claim by using a variety of different hypotheses to link evidence and theory. It is also important to test the hypotheses used in this linking. The holist is right to think that our faith in any particular claim depends upon our faith in the hypotheses we have used to link observation and theory, and that our faith in these hypotheses depends in turn upon further linking hypotheses. But this does not entail that a piece of evidence cannot bear on one part of a world-view without bearing on all of it. Neither does it entail that we cannot accept one claim a world-view makes without accepting all the claims it makes. Which claims are confirmed or disconfirmed, and to what degree, will depend both on the evidence and the structure of the world-view. [21]

Our present debate provides us with a good example. A theistic world-view maintains the reality of the material world and the physicalist will certainly side with the theist in this. However, he will scarcely agree that his believing this commits him to the truth of theism as a whole. The reason he will cite is that the theist, although he agrees with the physicalist in regarding the world as real, goes on to make some claims with which the physicalist does not agree, namely that the world, although real, was created by God and is subject to His influence. The physicalist will quite correctly point out that the claim that the material world is real does not entail the claim that it was created by God and that the evidence which confirms the former claim does not confirm the latter.

It is quite legitimate to accept well-tested portions of a world-view, yet reject other more speculative portions of it. Thus the theist is under no obligation to falsify all the claims of physicalism. He is at liberty to accept the better-tested portions of physicalism, yet reject the claim that energy can neither be created nor destroyed. It is possible, therefore, to conceive of an accumulation of evidence which would count not against the better-tested portions of physicalism, but against the strong form of the Principle of the Conservation of Energy.

My conclusion, then, is that empirical evidence is relevant to the issue of the truth of physicalism. It is relevant not in the sense that it could ever confirm physicalism, but in the sense that it could disconfirm it. The reason this is so is that a defining-postulate of physicalism, namely the claim that energy can neither be created nor destroyed, is a deep structural assumption which can never be established, but which can conceivably be disestablished.

Relevant though empirical evidence may be, it must nevertheless be emphasized that falsifying a world-view is not merely a matter of producing discordant evidence. In theory, physicalism would be disconfirmed if we could falsify the claim that energy can neither be created nor destroyed. Theoretically, it seems entirely conceivable that we might show that physicalism is an inadequate world-view, even if we have no alternative world-view to put in its place. In actual practice, the task is liable to prove considerably more difficult. Practically speaking, if we wish to falsify a world-view we must be prepared not only to make reference to a body of discordant data, but also to defend an alternative world-view capable of explaining that data.

The reason for this is that world-views have immense explanatory power, otherwise they could scarcely be termed world-views. This fact that they explain large areas of experience means that a world-view is rarely, if ever, abandoned merely because there exist some discordant data. Difficulties in a world-view do not generally persuade its adherents to abandon it, unless there exists a rival world-view which seems better able to resolve those difficulties. A world-view which accounts for a great deal of our experience is generally thought to be better than no theory at all. As Ian Barbour notes:

we should picture not a two-way confrontation of theory with falsifying data, but a three-way confrontation of rival theories with a body of data of varying degrees of susceptibility to reinterpretation ... Abandoning one set of fundamental beliefs ... involves at least implicit acknowledgment of possible alternatives even if one reserves judgment about them. [22]

In actual practice, therefore, evaluating the adequacy of physicalism as a world-view involves not merely examining its "fit" with the empirical data, but its "fit" as it compares to the "fit" of rivals such as theism.

This reveals the scope of the debate. The believer in miracles must be prepared to elaborate and defend an alternative world-view, namely theism. Otherwise, his claim that the strong form of the Principle of the Conservation of Energy is unconfirmed will be accorded little weight. In the absence of a rival world-view, the physicalist will exploit the distinction I drew between a belief which is confirmed and a belief which is plausible. He will argue that, even if it is not confirmed, the belief that energy can neither be created nor destroyed is plausible because there exists no rival view capable of explaining the truth of the weak form of the Principle of the Conservation of Energy.

The strategy of the theist, then, must be to argue that her world-view accounts not only for the large body of truth contained in physicalism, but also for that body of data which casts doubt on physicalism, namely the body of data which the theist takes to suggest the occurrence of miracles. She must show that it is possible to retain the best-tested parts of physicalism, yet reject it as an adequate world-view. In particular, she must show that it makes sense to accept the weak form of the Principle of the Conservation of Energy, yet reject its strong form. If she can do this she will be in a position to claim that belief in physicalism is not only unconfirmed, but implausible.

THE TASK OF THE THEIST

Successfully to challenge the physicalist the theist must accomplish three things. First, she must clarify and develop the idea of agency, since implicit in any defence of miracles is the notion of an immaterial agent with the ability to produce or influence events in the material world. If she can do this she will be in a position to sidestep entirely objections to miracles such as those of Nowell-Smith, who argues that the concept of the miraculous is a mere pseudo-concept with no real explanatory power. She will be able to show that these objections are erroneous because they implicitly assume there exists only one type of causality and consequently only one legitimate type of explanation.

Second, she must show that there is a body of evidence which supports her in postulating the existence of immaterial agents capable of influencing events in the material world. To refuse this challenge is to fall foul of the principle that we must not multiply entities needlessly. Unless the requirements of Occam's Razor can be met, the theist must cede the day to the physicalist. It should be noted, however, that part of the evidence she can conceivably point to are events which appear miraculous, that is to say events which are reasonably interpreted as miracles if we entertain theism as a hypothesis. As I noted earlier, links between evidence and theory can be established when a theory is tested without thereby presupposing the truth of that theory.

Third, the theist must show that her views concerning immaterial agents and agent causality are part of a larger system of thought which not only explains the body of data which physicalism does not explain, but also that the body of data which physicalism explains extremely well. She must develop her view in such a manner that it "corrects" physicalism, but does not totally repudiate it. She must develop, in other words, a world-view which accepts and explains all that is true in physicalism, yet provides a theoretical framework in which sense is made of the immaterial realities which physicalism refuses to countenance.

It is beyond the scope of this work to pronounce on whether, in fact, the theist can accomplish all this. Several remarks are in order, however, on what is involved in demonstrating these three things.

With regard to the task of clarifying and developing the notions of agent and agent causality, two very general comments need to be made. The first is that it is important that the theist show not only that we make reference to agents and agent causality in our everyday speech, but that these notions are "primitive," in the sense that they cannot be shown to be merely a convenient way of talking about non-teleological explanations. The second is that an analysis of other selves is of great relevance to this issue. Questions of whether we ascribe to other persons non-observable characteristics which transcend our direct experience of their bodies, and what it means to do this, will cast light on the notions of agent and agent causality. As I indicated earlier, the mind-body question is relevant to the issue of miracles.

Concerning the second task, I have said that it is important that the theist produce some positive evidence which justifies postulating the existence of immaterial agents. The subject of evidence and the principles by which it is assessed will be discussed in my next chapter so I need not say much about this task here. I do think it important, however, to note that it would not be fair for the physicalist to demand that the evidence the theist appeals to be experimentally reproducible. The reason is that the theist is committed to a non-regularity view of agent causality.[23] His strategy, therefore, must not be to attempt to discover experimentally reproducible evidence, but rather to point to explanatory hiatuses which cannot be satisfactorily explained except on the supposition of the operation of an immaterial agent or agents. This does not prevent him from appealing to physical evidence (for example, the regeneration of a lost limb might constitute evidence for a miracle), but it does mean that it would be unfair to demand that such a result be duplicated before it be accepted as evidence.

Finally, as regards his third task of showing that theism "corrects" physicalism, the theist must show that his world-view exhibits the twin virtues of consilience and simplicity. It is essential that it be consilient in that it needs to unify and systematize the facts it purports to explain. Moreover, to say a theory is consilient is to say more than that it "fits the facts," that it is formally consistent with their truth; rather, "it is to say first that the theory explains the facts, and second that the facts it explains are taken from more than one domain."[24] It is not enough for a world-view to be consilient, however. The theist must also show that theism is simple in the sense that it explains the facts without making a lot of *ad hoc* assumptions. I wish to emphasize that to say that theism must be simple in this sense is in no way to suggest that it cannot be ontologically complex. As Paul Thagard comments,

[we are] not to multiply entities beyond necessity. Necessity is a function of the range of facts to be explained without the use of a lot of auxiliary assumptions. Ontological complexity does not detract from the explanatory value or acceptability of a theory so long as the complexity contributes towards consilience and simplicity.[25]

It also bears emphasizing that, although these three tasks may be separated in theory, they are inextricably entwined in practice. It is tempting to think that the person who believes in miracles must proceed by first elaborating and analysing the concept of agency, then inquiring whether there is any evidence to suggest the existence of an immaterial agent or agents and finally, having done all this, attempt to integrate the notion of the miraculous into theism as a consilient and simple world-view. In practice, though, his concept of what an agent is and how agent causality functions cannot be arrived at independently of interacting with the evidence he takes to support him in postulating another type of substance and causality. Equally, his assessment of evidence does not take place in a vacuum, but is influenced by his world-view. This, as I have said, in no implies that his views are unfalsifiable. We have already seen in our discussion of world-views and the possibility of falsifyng a world-view that the fact that concepts, evidence, and theory are linked together does not imply a holistic view of theorizing.

Demonstrating these three things is a large and complex undertaking. So great and complicated is it that, strictly speaking, it is inaccurate to speak of the task of the person who wishes to defend theism; rather, we should speak of the collective task of people who wish to defend theism. Similarly, we should speak not of the task of the person who wishes to defend physicalism, but of the collective task of people who wish to defend physicalism. The elaboration and defence of a world-view presupposes a community of scholars: a community in which various members, sharing a common faith that their world-view may indeed be elaborated and defended, undertake different projects directed towards this goal. World-views, at least in some senses, constitute research traditions within which communities of scholars work.[26] Such a community has a commitment to a certain traditional body of thought and adheres very tenaciously to its world-view, preferring to explore its potentialities rather than prematurely abandoning it in the face of difficulties judged more apparent than real. Except in extreme cases, this tenacity does not deserve to be censured. It is hard to see how knowledge could advance if it did not exist. As Imre Lakatos notes,

the idea of instant rationality ... [is] utopian ... [All] theories of
instant rationality – and instant learning – fail ... [R]ationality
works much slower than most people tend to think.[27]

But the existence of this tenacity highlights an important
fact: there inevitably exist what may be termed metaphysical predilections that influence our assessment of
data. Care must be taken that these predilections do not
lead to a premature rejection of alternative interpretations
suggested by rival world-views and thus degenerate into an
unreasoning dogmatism.

Consider, for instance, the treatment of historical
documents containing accounts of miracles, say the gospels
of the New Testament. By virtue of her world-view, the
physicalist is inclined to reject the claim that miracles
occur. Thus, she questions the historical accuracy of any
document which contains an account of miracles. There is
nothing wrong in her insistence that we assess the accuracy
of such documents. Indeed, such insistence is necessary if
we are to guard against an easy credulity. What deserves
emphasis, however, is that her assessment of these documents must be based on features other than the fact that
they contain accounts of miracles. It will not do for her to
assume that any account of a miracle must be unhistorical.
Unless it can be buttressed with independent arguments,
such as assessment amounts to mere dogmatism.

The fundamental aim of criticism must be not to presuppose a system into which evidence is either forced or else
discarded, but to arrive at a coherent account which does
justice to it. Granted world-views influence how evidence
gets viewed, nevertheless evidence may have implications
concerning the adequacy of a particular world-view. Both
the theist and the physicalist must remember that world-
views are to fit the evidence – explain the evidence and at
the same time exhibit the twin virtues of consiliency and
simplicity, not serve as beds of Procrustes to force it into
alien categories.

CHAPTER SEVEN

Miracles and Evidence

In the preceding chapter I argued that those who defend belief in miracles must do so within the context of a theistic world-view. I also argued that, contrary to a good deal of contemporary thinking, world-views are falsifiable. Neither the fact that there exist no privileged analytic truths connecting the language of evidence with the language of theory nor the fact that a world-view may be made consistent with any body of evidence, provided we are prepared to indulge in enough *ad hoc* tinkering, implies that world-views cannot be falsified. Although it is difficult to specify an event or set of events that would falsify a given world-view conclusively, it is nevertheless true that empirical data is relevant to the question of the truth of a world-view and serves to render it more or less plausible. Proponents of different world-views, therefore, are not imprisoned in intellectual ghettos. Commitment to a particular world-view does not imply that we cannot understand or assess systems of thought other than our own.

I argued that those who believe in miracles must show three things: first, that the notions of an immaterial agent and agent causality are coherent and not mere pseudo-concepts; second, that there is a positive body of evidence which supports them in postulating the existence of immaterial agents and agent causality; finally that theism swallows up physicalism, so to speak, for it explains all that physicalism explains and more. If they can accomplish these three things they will be in a position not only to hold that belief in physicalism is unconfirmed, but that it is implausible.

In this chapter I propose to examine the second of these tasks in more detail. I want to say something about the various types of evidence the believer might appeal to and the principles governing assessment of this evidence. I should like then to describe the type and degree of evidence necessary to justify belief in a miracle. Finally, although I do not intend to involve myself in the apologetic endeavour of arguing that there is sufficient evidence to justify belief in miracles, I want to comment briefly on the arguments in Part II of Hume's essay, where he attempts to demonstrate that the actual evidence in favour of miracles is very poor.

TYPES OF EVIDENCE AND PRINCIPLES OF ASSESSMENT

Before directly discussing the issue of evidence and its assessment, I want to dispose of a psychologically seductive, but simplistic, approach to the problem. Many critics, among them Hume, argue that, since the class of non-miraculous events far outnumbers the class of miraculous events, the probability that a miracle occurred in a particular instance will always be vastly lower than the probability that some non-miraculous event took place. Thus, when we come to assess reports of a miracle, we must always conclude that it is very improbable that the miracle actually occurred.

Superficially, this is an elegant and powerful argument. However, to employ it is to be guilty not only of the fallacy of division, but of attempting to resolve a factual matter by means of definition. From the mere fact that one class contains a great many more members than another we can conclude very little. No theist would want to say that the class of events properly called miracles approaches the size of the class of non-miraculous events, but that does not mean that the probability that any particular miracle occurred is low. It is impossible to determine the existential status of a conceivable event simply by considering the numerical size of the class to which it belongs.[1] Rather, it must be determined in relation to all the evidence relevant to that event. To think otherwise would be to rule out not only miracles, but any number of well-established non-miraculous, but nevertheless rare, events. All that can be established by comparing the sizes of the two classes is that non-miraculous events are more common than miracles. This is scarcely at issue, however. The question is not how common are miracles, but what would constitute evidence for a miracle. It is to this question I turn.

There are, I think, three basic types of evidence that are relevant to establishing the occurrence of a miracle. These are: (1) personal observation; (2) relevant physical traces; and (3) the testimony of others. Some philosophers would want to insist that this list is too short. Swinburne, for example, insists there exists a fourth type of evidence, namely "our contemporary understanding of what things are physically impossible or improbable."[2] He admits that this fourth type differs from the other types of evidence in that it functions "only [as] a corrective to the other three, not [as] an independent source of detailed information."[3] He contends, however, that it is relevant to assessing whether a miracle has occurred. In Swinburne's view, positive evidence from the other three sources must be weighed against this fourth type which suggests that miracles are either impossible or very improbable. If belief in a miracle is to be justified then the evidence from the first three sources must outweigh the negative evidence from the fourth.

I think Swinburne's claim mistaken. It is quite true that in order to call an event a miracle we must have good reason to think it is an event beyond the power of an unaided nature to produce. It is also quite true that our judgment on this presupposes a knowledge of the laws of nature. But it is not true that the laws of nature make any event either impossible or improbable. Our judgment concerning this will depend not upon our knowledge of the laws of nature, but upon our world-view. For example, we saw earlier that, although the laws of nature indicate that virgins do not conceive unless nature is overridden in some way, they do not entail that such an event cannot happen or is antecedently improbable. How probable we think such an event is depends upon how likely we think it is that a transcendent agent will override nature in such a way as to produce it. Swinburne is wrong, therefore, to take for granted that there exists a homogeneous understanding of what things are physically impossible or improbable. World-views influence how we evaluate evidence, but they cannot themselves be considered a part of the evidence.

Given that these three types of evidence are relevant to the question whether miracles occur, there remain questions of how evidence is to be assessed. What general principles govern our assessment of the evidence?

It might be maintained that this question can be answered very quickly and easily. The most basic and fundamental principle can be stated quite simply: we ought to accept as much evidence as is possible and yet develop a coherent account consistent with the evidence. Things are not quite so simple, however. Although this principle is basic and we utilize it in all areas of our lives, there are several subsidiary limiting principles which make its application quite complicated in practice.

One of the most important of these is that different types of evidence must be weighted differently. Some types of evidence are intrinsically more valuable than others. For example, one's own apparent memory of an event ought, *prima facie*, to be given more weight than the testimony of another witness. It usually makes more sense to suppose that someone may be lying than to believe one's memory to be mistaken. My use of the phrases *prima facie* and *usually* is deliberate. Clearly, there are considerations which could justify the conclusion that another's testimony should be weighted more heavily than one's own apparent memory. The realization that, in a certain situation, one was coping with a great deal of stress, for instance, might persuade one that the testimony of others is to be preferred to one's own apparent memory. However, in the absence of such considerations, and in view of the fact that memory tends to provide clues by which to weigh itself, it seems clear that one's apparent memories are to be weighted more heavily than the testimony of others.

Another important subsidiary principle is that particular evidences must be accorded different weights on the basis of the empirical evidence available concerning their reliability. This is accomplished by a procedure which we may term "narrowing the evidence class."[4] Thus, if we wish to evaluate the testimony of an individual we do not exclusively investigate the worth of testimony in general, but also consider the worth of the individual's testimony in particular. With good reason, we consider that the testimony of a person who has been reliable in the past should be weighted more heavily than the testimony of someone who has been unreliable. It should be noted that this procedure presupposes the general reliability of other evidence, since it is only by accepting this reliability that we can arrive at an independent basis by which to evaluate the particular piece of evidence in question. This means that this principle, although very useful, is somewhat limited. For unless we are prepared to deal with an infinite regress of evidences, we must admit there is some evidence which ought to be accepted even without further evidence in its favour. As Swinburne puts it,

the testing of evidence of one class can only be performed if we presuppose the reliability in general of other evidence ... We may have empirical evidence about the reliability of other evidence, but as such evidence will consist of more empirical evidence, we have to stop somewhere, with evidence which we can take to be reliable without empirical evidence thereof.[5]

The final subsidiary principle I wish to note is that we ought not to reject coincident evidence, unless we can give a satisfactory explanation of why it should coincide. If various pieces of evidence, either of one type or of various types, coincide, this constitutes a strong reason for accepting them. For example, if a number of witnesses agree in their testimony, or if their testimony agrees with the evidence derived from physical traces, we become much more sure that the evidence is reliable and ought to be accepted. The only time this does not happen is when we have reason to think there exists some alternative explanation of why the evidence coincides. We may, for example, uncover further evidence which leads us to suspect collusion among the witnesses, or that the physical traces in question have been "cooked." When this happens, coincidence, far from being a reason to accept the evidence, is a reason to reject it. Like the others, this principle is simple enough in theory, but complex in application. We expect independent witnesses of an event to agree on its major details, but not necessarily to agree upon, or even report the same, minor details. Just how much agreement and how much disagreement we should expect, however, is no simple matter and will vary with each case. All that can be said in general is that if multiple reports of a miracle exhibit both the agreement as regards the major details of the event and the diversity concerning minor details that is characteristic of independent reports of the same event then coincident evidence must be heavily weighted.

We have discussed the types of evidence relevant to establishing whether a miracle occurred and the principles by which this evidence is assessed. It is time to say something about the amount and type of evidence needed to justify belief in a miracle. I think there can be no question that it is at least conceivable that there might exist sufficient evidence to justify believe in a miracle. For example, if we were to witness and film the instantaneous regrowth of a man's withered arm, knowing that both the man and his friends were religious people of exemplary character who had been praying for just this event, we would surely be justified in believing that the event had actually occurred and was a miracle. Equally, it must be admitted that to leave the matter at this is not to have said a great deal. By their very nature, miracles are not common occurrences. They are not events, therefore, that most people could expect to observe directly. Even if we suppose that some people are so privileged, they can never observe more than a small portion of the miracles reported throughout history.

Evidence from physical traces, of course, is relevant, but it will not do to expect too much from this source. In general, physical traces tend to disappear with the passage of time. There is also the problem that, even when the event in question is fairly recent, physical traces generally need to be supplemented with testimonial evidence. It is hard to conceive of a set of circumstances in which the occurrence of a miracle could be established on the basis of physical traces alone. This is not to say that physical traces do not have an important role in evaluating accounts of miracles. In more recent instances they may persuade us that something remarkable did indeed happen and that it needs explanation. We might find, say, that a man who was born without an arm, a fact we might have established through personal observation or through testimonial evidence, now has an arm. In the case of more remote events it is often possible on the basis of physical traces to establish whether the report is accurate as concerns historical, cultural, and geographical detail. In such instances, physical traces can serve as a negative test for the truth of the miracle-claim. They establish not that the miracle actually occurred, but that the report of its occurrence is accurate and trustworthy in other respects.

Given the limitations of these other two types of evidence, the important question is whether testimonial evidence alone can justify belief in miracles. If it can, then how much testimonial evidence is necessary?

Some philosophers, notably Antony Flew, deny the possibility that testimonial evidence could justify belief in miracles. He argues that

the criteria by which we must assess historical testimony, and the general presumptions which alone make it possible for us to construct the detritus of the past as historical evidence, must inevitably rule out any possibility of establishing upon purely historical grounds, that some genuinely miraculous event has indeed occurred.[6]

Flew's argument in support of this conclusion amounts to the following: (1) historical investigation presupposes the truth of the laws of nature; (2) the laws of nature must be defined as exceptionless; and (3) miracles must be defined in terms of inconsistency with the laws of nature.[7] This argument is valid, but not sound. Leaving aside discussion of Flew's first two premises, his third premise cannot be defended. Fundamental to the concept of miracle is the idea that nature must be overridden if a miracle is to occur. But Flew is mistaken in thinking that this implies that the laws of nature must be violated if a miracle occurs. As I have already shown, miracles, considered as objective events specially caused by God, can conceivably occur in a world which behaves, always and everywhere, completely in accordance with the laws of nature.

Elsewhere, Flew offers another argument in support of his view that testimonial evidence could never justify belief in a miracle. It takes the form of a balance-of-probabilities argument based on the presumption that, in principle, the evidence in favour of an event like a miracle can never outweigh the evidence in favour of a law of nature. He writes,

The justification for giving the "scientific" ... ultimate precedence ... over the "historical" lies in the nature of the propositions concerned and in the evidence which can be deployed to sustain them. It derives – to borrow the expression of Hume's material mode of thought – "from the very nature of the fact." The candidate historical proposition will be particular, often singular, and in the past tense ... by reason of this very pastness and particularity it is no longer possible for anyone to examine the subject directly for himself ...

The "law of nature" will, unlike the candidate historical proposition, be a general nomological. It can thus in theory – though obviously not always in practice – be tested at any time by any person.[8]

Two comments are in order here. First, Flew's belief that propositions expressing scientific laws are always open to testing whereas propositions reporting historical events are not is mistaken. As Swinburne comments:

Particular experiments on particular occasions only give a certain and far from conclusive support to claims that a purported scientific law is true. Any person can test for the truth of a purported scientific law, but a positive result to one test will give only limited support to the claim. Exactly the same holds for purported historical truths. Anyone can examine the evidence, but a particular piece of evidence gives only limited support to the claim that the historical proposition is true. But in the historical as in the scientific case, there is no limit to the testing which we can do. We can go on and on testing for the truth of historical as of scientific propositions. True, the actual traces, apparent memories and testimony ... available to an inquirer are unlikely to increase in number ... But although the number of pieces of direct evidence about what happened may not increase, more and more evidence can be obtained about the reliability of the evidence which we have. One could show the evidence yielded by traces of certain types, or testimony given by witnesses of such-and-such character in such-and-such circumstances was always correct. This indirect evidence could mount up in just the way in which the evidence of the physical impossibility of an event could mount up.[9]

Second, even if Flew could establish his view that belief in the laws of nature is more firmly established than belief in particular historical events, his conclusion still does not follow. In order to make his argument work he must show two things. He must show not only that the evidence in favour of the laws of nature outweighs the evidence in favour of miracles, but that there exists a conflict between these two bodies of evidence. This latter task cannot be accomplished. Only if miracles imply violations of the laws of nature does there exist conflict between the evidence which establishes belief in these laws and the evidence which establishes belief in miracles. Given that miracles need not be so defined, Flew's argument fails.

This suggests a curious reversal of what is usually thought to be the case. Usually the burden of proof in this matter is thought to lie squarely on the shoulders of the theist. It is thought that the theist must show that, in spite of a miracle's antecedent improbability, there is sufficient evidence to justify belief in it. In reality, exactly the opposite holds true. The basic principle of accepting as much evidence as is consistent with developing a coherent account implies that, in the absence of contrary evidence or a stronger body of contrary evidence, testimonial evidence can justify belief in a miracle. It is not the theist who must justify accepting reports of miracles, but the physicalist who must justify rejecting them.

HUME'S A POSTERIORI ARGUMENTS

The conclusion we have reached is that testimonial evidence could conceivably justify belief in miracles and that, since there is no necessary conflict between evidence which justifies belief in a miracle and evidence which justifies belief in the laws of nature, the amount needed is not nearly so great as is sometimes thought. It is at this point that examination of Hume's *a posteriori* arguments found in Part II of his essay becomes relevant. By these arguments, Hume thought he could show that whether or not it is theoretically possible that testimonial evidence might be sufficiently strong to justify belief in miracles, in actual fact the evidence that exists is so poor that it cannot even begin to serve as grounds for belief in miracles. Although it is not my purpose to debate whether in fact there is sufficient evidence to justify belief in miracles, I think it is important to evaluate Hume's negative claim that there is not.

As has been frequently noted, the first *a posteriori* argument is not so much an argument as "a categorical denial that there has ever in fact been a case in which various specified requirements have been met, and where the evidence has been sufficient to justify belief [in miracles]."[10] Hume writes that

there is not to be found, in all history, any miracle attested by a sufficient number of men of such unquestioned good sense, education and learning as to secure us against all delusion in themselves, of such undoubted integrity as to place them beyond all suspicion of any design to deceive others ...[11]

It is important to notice that Hume seems to have the New Testament documents in mind and many of his points are directed at Christian apologists of the day who stressed the reliability of the various Apostles as witnesses. As Burns notes, "far from being an inventory of the requirements in principle necessarily required in order to establish any reported fact with 'full assurance', and which happen, simply as a matter of fact, never to have been fulfilled in the case of miracles, the list is an *ad hoc* compilation specifically directed against the credentials of the Apostles as witnesses."[12] Moreover, even accepting the unrealistic standards of evidence that Hume demands, the argument depends on a factual claim that is very dubious. Hume admits this himself. He writes concerning the Jansenist miracles:

There surely never was a greater number of miracles ascribed to one person than those which were lately said to have been wrought in France upon the tomb of Abbé Paris, the famous Jansenist with whose sanctity the people were so long deluded ... [W]hat is extraordinary is that many of the miracles were immediately proved upon the spot, before judges of unquestioned integrity, attested by witnesses of credit and distinction, in a learned age on the most eminent theatre that is now in the world.[13]

Hume's reply to his own example, it ought to be emphasized, was not to demonstrate that the evidence in favour of these miracles was not so good as it first appears, but a dogmatic assertion that miracles cannot occur. All he says concerning the example is this: "And what have we to oppose to such a cloud of witnesses but the absolute impossibility or miraculous nature of the events which they relate."[14]

Flew attempts to escape the conclusion that Hume retreats into dogmatism at this point by interpreting his use of the word *impossibility* to refer to physical as opposed to logical impossibility. Against the charge that this makes Hume guilty either of maintaining that something which is conceivable is nevertheless impossible or that the notion of a miracle is a mere pseudo-concept, neither of which was Hume's official view, Flew claims that Hume was arguing defensively, showing the problems in rival viewpoints, rather than offensively.[15] Leaving aside the fact that this seems an unduly charitable reading of Hume, the fact remains that even on this reading, Hume does not so much defend the argument as abandon it. He does not contest the fact that this argument is based on a dubious factual claim. At best, his remarks can be seen as a retreat to his *a priori* argument of Part I, namely that belief in miracles can never be justified on the basis of testimony.

Hume's second argument in Part II is, essentially, that whenever a miracle story is told in a religious context its credibility is nil.

[I]f the spirit of religion joins itself to the love of wonder, there is an end of common sense, and human testimony in these circumstances loses all pretensions to authority. A religionist may be an enthusiast and imagine he sees what has not reality, he may know his narrative to be false and yet persevere in it with the best intentions in the world for the sake of promoting so holy a cause.[16]

This argument has little to recommend it. I do not think any one would dispute the fact that it is sometimes the case that when "the spirit of religion joins itself to the love of wonder there is an end of common sense." However, to make this claim universal it needs to be argued in greater detail than Hume in fact does. It is not at all clear that religious people who report first-hand experience of miracles invariably suffer from a deficiency of common sense or an undue credulity and love of wonder. In many cases it seems very difficult to impugn either their common sense or honesty.[17]

In fact it seems possible to argue that at least in some cases religious belief may militate against any easy acceptance of miracles. One of Hume's most capable early critics, George Campbell, speaking of the worth of the Apostles' testimony for Christ's miracles, makes this point when he suggests that Hume overlooked the fact that

the prejudice resulting from the religious affection, may just as readily obstruct as promote our faith in a ... miracle. What things in nature are more contrary than one religion to another ...? If the faith of the witnesses stood originally in opposition to the doctrine attested by the miracles; if the only account that can be given of their conversion, is the conviction which the miracles produced in them ... [then we have] a very strong presumption in favour of that evidence.[18]

Hume's third *a posteriori* argument is that reports of miracles must be rejected because they come down to us from ancient times. He writes that

it forms a strong presumption against all supernatural and miraculous relations that they are observed chiefly to abound among ignorant and barbarous nations; or if a civilized people has ever given admission to any of them, that people will be found to have received them from ignorant and barbarous ancestors who transmitted them with that inviolable sanction and authority which always attend received opinions.[19]

Again, this is a very weak argument. His factual claim that reports of miracles are not found among well-educated civilized people, or that if they are they are invariably received from ignorant and barbarous ancestors, is simply false.[20] Although counter-examples in our own day may be cited, his own example concerning the tomb of the Abbé Paris seems adequate to dispose of the factual claim put forward in this argument. Hume must have been aware that he was putting forward a factual claim which required further argument.

Indeed, even if it were found to be true that reports of miracles are found chiefly among ignorant and barbarous people the argument would still be suspect. Hume's unstated premise appears to be that people who lived long before the rise of science were insufficiently acquainted with the course of nature to distinguish a miracle from a natural event. This is only superficially plausible. Joseph did not have to have the detailed knowledge of modern biologists to know that virgins do not conceive in the normal course of events and the disciples did not have to have a knowledge of modern physics to realize that multiplication of loaves and fishes does not occur in the normal course of nature. Simply because a report of a miracle comes from an earlier age does not therefore mean that it can be disregarded.

Finally, it should be noted that, just as there is no *a priori* reason for contending that because some reports of miracles are lies and fabrications all reports of miracles may be rejected, there is no *a priori* reason to suppose that all ages should be equally endowed with miracles. Whether or not miracles occur equally in all ages, and whether or not all reports of miracles are fabrications, are questions concerning matters of fact and must be investigated empirically, not legislated *a priori*. Provided there is good evidence for their occurrence, the fact that more miracles are reported in one period of history than another constitutes no reason for disbelief.

Hume's fourth *a posteriori* argument is more interesting than his first three. Its aim, like his *a priori* argument in Part I, is to discredit any presumed evidence for a miracle by pointing to a conflict of evidence which destroys the force of the presumed evidence in favour of the miracle. He takes as his starting point the fact that reports of miracles occur in a great many religions. He argues that

in destroying a rival system ... a miracle likewise destroys the credit of those miracles on which that system was established, so that all the prodigies of different religions are to be regarded as contrary facts, and the evidences of these prodigies, whether weak or strong, as opposite each other.[21]

Although this argument is scarcely original, having long been used by the Deists prior to Hume's adoption of it, it is very interesting and, at first glance, powerful. This, combined with Hume's penchant for Pyrrhonistic paradox, may well explain its inclusion in the essay. However, despite its initial formidable appearance, closer inspection reveals at least two major weaknesses.

First, although he does talk of weak and strong evidence for individual miracles, Hume seems to assume that the body of evidence supporting belief in the miracles of one religion can be no greater than the body of evidence supporting belief in the miracles of some a certain religion. There is no *a priori* reason why this should be so. If in fact the evidence for miracles in a certain religion is very strong and the evidence for miracles in other religions is very weak, there exists no reason for seriously questioning the strongly evidenced claims.

Second, the argument contains a suppressed premise, namely that miracles only occur in connection with the religion whose system of theology contains the most truth and that the chief purpose of a miracle is to guarantee the truth of that system of theology. Given that Hume was concerned to "establish it as a maxim that no human testimony can have such force as to prove a miracle and make it a just foundation for any ... system of religion,"[22] it is understandable that he would assume the truth of this premise. It is, however, a dubious one. At least so far as Christianity is concerned, it is a mistake to think that the sole or even chief purpose of a miracle is to guarantee the truth of the system of theology with which it is associated. Equally, very few theologians would be prepared to suggest that God is not active in religions other than Christianity. In at least one case, then, Hume is forced to admit there is no compelling reason why the believer cannot hold that miracles occur in more than one religion and therefore, *a fortiori*, there is no compelling reason why the believer should regard the evidence for such miracles as "contrary facts."

Hume's *a posteriori* arguments, no less than his *a priori* argument, fail to achieve their aim. They do not establish the conclusion that the actual testimonial evidence is so poor that it cannot serve as ground for a rationally justified belief in the occurrence of miracles.

CHAPTER EIGHT

Miracles and Apologetics

In this final chapter I wish to discuss the issue of miracles and their apologetic significance. Since I am a Christian and persuaded of the truth of my beliefs, my remarks will bear most directly on the concerns of the Christian apologist.

CHANGING VIEWS ON THE APOLOGETIC SIGNIFICANCE OF MIRACLES

The argument that miracles help to establish the truth of theism in general and Christianity in particular was once very popular. Indeed, the debate surrounding it was a dominant feature of English intellectual life early in the eighteenth century, when "almost every English theologian, philosopher, or even simply man of letters ... made some contribution to it."[1] Interestingly, those who defended the apologetic importance of miracles "were ... also prominently involved in the development of the scientific outlook which lay behind the achievements of late seventeenth-century English science."[2]

In the last two centuries, however, there has been an increasing tendency to see miracles as having little or no apologetic value. Indeed, some thinkers see them as an obstacle to belief and feel there is a need to strip Christianity of its miraculous elements so as to demythologize it and make it relevant to modern man. Thus Rudolph Bultmann spoke for a great many scholars when he argued that

[i]t is impossible to use electric light and the wireless and to avail ourselves of modern medical and surgical discoveries, and at the same time to believe in the New Testament world of spirits and miracles.[3]

Even those of more conservative bent, concerned to retain belief in miracles, often see them as an embarrassment, something that makes their task more difficult than it would otherwise be. In a recent issue of the *Journal of the American Scientific Affiliation*, devoted entirely to the topic of miracles and their relation to science, Stephen Wykstra contributed an article entitled "The Problem of Miracle in the Apologetic from History" in which he examines the question whether miracles have any apologetic value. What he suggests we find is that those who defend the apologetic importance of miracles employ normal procedures when estimating the probability of naturalistic alternative hypotheses, but abstain from these procedures when gauging the probability of a miracle. His conclusion is that, unless the apologist is prepared to defend "a policy of systematic inconsistency with respect to the probability-estimating procedures he employs" – a prospect which he admits is not bright – it is a mistake to think miracles have any apologetic value.[4] Indeed, although Wykstra is careful not to draw this conclusion, his argument seems to imply that miracles are an apologetic liability.

I think the unwillingness of modern theists to see miracles as an apologetic asset is mistaken. By way of demonstrating this, I want to discuss three topics: the role of miracles in demonstrating the superiority of theism over physicalism; their part in deciding between theism and rival world-views other than physicalism; and whether miracles can confirm only theism in general or Christianity in particular.

I want to begin by saying that I accept the view of most contemporary apologists that to call an event a miracle is to presuppose the truth of theism. But I do not accept the common assumption that it is a consequence of this view that an event we are prepared to call a miracle cannot serve as independent evidence for God's existence. I think this assumption is erroneous and arises through conflating two related, but quite distinct, questions. The first is whether once we attach the label "miracle" to an event we are committed to the truth of theism. The second is whether in deciding if we ought to apply the label, we must presuppose the truth of theism.

Both questions are important, but I shall postpone my discussion of the former until later in the chapter where I examine the relation of theism to rival world-views other than physicalism. The point I want to make in the present discussion is that even if we hold that we are committed to theism once we call an event a miracle, this in no way entails that we must be committed to theism before we can decide whether it meets the criteria by which we determine if it is best seen as a miracle or a mere anomaly of nature.

At the risk of being redundant, I want to emphasize that we do not need to believe that theism is true before we can decide whether or not we should label an event a miracle. Assuming there is good evidence that an unusual event occurred, we are quite at liberty to draw upon the concepts of theism in attempting to explain it, even if we do not as yet accept the truth of theism. As I argued in chapter six, the links between theory and evidence can be supplied by the theory to be tested, so long as these links are not used in such a way as to guarantee that the theory will be positively instantiated whatever the evidence. In other words, all that is required is that we entertain theism as a hypothesis, and consider whether the event is best explained by the theistic hypothesis or by some rival hypothesis. If it is best explained by the theistic hypothesis then it constitutes independent evidence for the superiority of theism over physicalism.

Note that I am not suggesting that claims that an event is a miracle are incorrigible. Nor am I suggesting that it will always be easy or even possible to decide whether an event is a miracle. We may be unsure whether the criteria for calling an event a miracle have been fulfilled. All that I am claiming is that, although all beliefs concerning matters of fact are corrigible, we might have good reason to call certain events miracles and that if this is the case then these events constitute independent evidence for the existence of God.

What I am proposing is that we treat physicalism and theism as analogous to large-scale scientific theories. In science an event is taken as independent evidence for a theory if it is easily accounted for by the theory, but proves an intractable problem for rival theories. Similarly, if an event can be satisfactorily explained by theism as being a miracle, but physicalism can offer no satisfactory explanation of it, then we are justified in seeing it as independent evidence for the superiority of theism over physicalism. Indeed, it is precisely events that can be satisfactorily explained by one world-view but not by a competing one which count towards establishing that world-view. Seen in this light, miracles, far from being an apologetic liability, are an asset, since it is precisely in its ability to account for these events that theism demonstrates its superiority.

Faced with this challenge, the physicalist may respond in either of two ways. First, at a theoretical level, he may argue that there are logical difficulties in appealing to the notion of the miraculous. Second, at a practical level, he may argue that what the theist takes as good evidence for the occurrence of a miracle is suspect.

Considering first the theoretical level, we have already noted the inadequacies of a number of the standard objections. For the sake of completeness, I want to discuss two objections I have not previously examined. They were briefly mentioned when I discussed Christine Overall's claim that miracles constitute cognitive evils; they deserve extended treatment, however.

Miracles and Moral Evil

One objection that is sometimes raised is that miracles, if they occur, make life more difficult for the theist because they enlarge and deepen the problem of evil. Once we take seriously the possibility that miracles occur, Herbert Burhenn says, we must "ask why an omnipotent God does not accomplish more and more good miraculously, or why he did not create a better world which would not require miraculous intervention to correct its faults."[5] As in the case of Overall, we are faced with an argument that miracles provide evidence against the existence of God.

The argument is psychologically persuasive: once we agree that God intervenes on some occasions to change the course of natural events we are only too inclined to ask why He does not intervene on other occasions. However, it is fallacious. An event is called a miracle if it can be seen to be religiously significant, if it can be seen to accord with what we conceive to be God's purposes. Now either the existence of evil in the world proves that God – conceived as being perfectly good and omnipotent – does not exist or it does not. If it proves God does not exist then there is no need to consider the issue of miracles; if it does not then it is hard to see how a lessening of evil in the world, – the healing of a child, say – can be seen as intensifying the problem of evil.

True, the theist may not be able to say why God heals a child in one case, but allows nature to take its course in another. This, however, is not to say that God does not have a morally sufficient reason for performing a miracle in one case and not another. The general strategy of the theist in dealing with the problem of evil is not to argue that we know the morally sufficient reason for the existence of every evil, but that we know the morally sufficient reasons which explain the existence of some evils and that there is good evidence for thinking that, although we do not know them, there exist morally sufficient reasons for the existence of all other evils. Providing this general strategy can be defended, there is no reason to think the occurrence of miracles poses the theist any special problems. Indeed, they may provide him with further resources. If miracles can be demonstrated, they absolve God of the charge of being an "absentee landlord," entirely unconcerned with the fate of His creation.

The physicalist might be tempted to reply that this is all very well in principle, but that in actual practice the events the theist appeals to as miracles cannot, without special pleading, be seen to be religiously significant. Two points must be remembered, however. The first is that the physicalist must proceed case by case; this approach cannot be used to justify any wholesale *a priori* rejection of purportedly miraculous events. Second, it is scarcely likely to succeed. Debate about events such as the Virgin Birth, the feeding of the multitudes, the healing of the sick and the Resurrection, to name only a few, focuses on whether these events actually occurred, not whether they are religiously significant. Even the most practised sceptic will admit that if these events occurred they can easily be seen to be religiously significant.

A more modest proposal would be to claim that some events theist have traditionally claimed to be miracles cannot easily be understood to have religious significance. This might prove to be true, but I do not think it helps the physicalist's cause much for two reasons. First, it would do little damage to the theist's argument if it were to be shown that there is a class of events which have mistakenly been called miracles. All that this would demonstrate is the worth of the criteria he proposed for distinguishing miraculous from non-miraculous events. Second, it does not follow from the fact that an event cannot easily be understood to have religious significance that it does not have such significance. The critic must at least admit the possibility that the event has religious significance, even if she has failed to perceive it. Finally, and most importantly, there is no reason to think that all miracles need be equally plausible or of equal apologetic value. As Newman remarks, the miracles which cannot easily be seen to have religious significance

are but a few in the midst of an overpowering majority consistently pointing to one grand object; they must not be torn from their moral context, but, on the credit of the rest, they must be considered but apparent exceptions ... It is obvious that a large system must consist of various parts of unequal utility and excellence; and to expect each particular occurrence to be complete in itself, is as unreasonable as to require the parts of some complicated machine, separately taken, to be all equally finished and fit for display.[6]

Further, it behooves the physicalist to proceed with epistemological humility when advancing the claim that certain events traditionally conceived as miracles cannot be understood as having religious significance. Consider, for example, the seemingly embarrassing incident of Jesus cursing the barren fig tree (Mark 11:12ff). Earlier writers, especially Thomas Woolston, took great pains to point out the apparent petulance and irrationality displayed by Jesus in this incident:

[I]f Jesus was frustrated of a long'd-for Meal of Figs, what need he have so reveng'd the Disappointment on the ... sinless and faultless Tree? ... If he was of Power to provide Bread for others on a sudden, he might sure have supply'd his own Necessities, and so have kept his Temper, without breaking into a violent Fit of Passion, upon present Want and Disappointment.

But what is yet worse, the Time of Figs was not yet, when Jesus look'd and long'd for them. Did ever any one hear or read of anything more ... unreasonable than for a Man to expect Fruit out of Season. Jesus could not but know this before he came to the Tree, and if he had had any Consideration, he would not have expected Figs on it ... How Jesus salved his Credit upon this his wild Prank; and prevented the Laughter of the Scribes and Pharisees upon it, I know not; but I cannot think of this Part of the letter of this Story, without smiling at it at this Day; and wonder our Divines are not laugh'd out of Countenance for reading it gravely, and having Jesus in Admiration for it. [7]

Confident that this event cannot be seen as religiously significant, Woolston charges that it throws suspicion upon Jesus' other miracles for

cursing the Figtree in this Fashion spoils the Credit, and sullies the Glory of his other Miracles. It has in its own Nature of such a malevolent Aspect, that its enough to make us suspect the Beneficience of Christ in his other Works, and to question whether there might not be some latent Poyson and diabolical Design under the Colour of his fairer Pretences to Almighty Power. [8]

Woolston seems to have a powerful case. How could such an apparently irrational and childish action have religious significance? Further study, however, reveals that his criticisms are misinformed. As F.F. Bruce comments,

a closer acquaintance with fig trees would have prevented ... [much] misunderstanding. "The time of figs was not yet," says Mark, for it was just before Passover, about six weeks before the fully-formed fig appears. The fact that Mark adds these words shows that he knew what he was talking about. When the fig-leaves appear about the end of March they are accompanied by a crop of small knobs, called taqsh by the Arabs, a sort of fore-runner of the real figs. These taqsh are eaten by peasants and others when hungry. They drop off before the real fig is formed. But if the leaves appear unaccompanied by taqsh, there will be no figs that year. So it was evident to our Lord, when He turned aside to see if there were any of these taqsh on the fig-tree to assuage His hunger for the time being, that the absence of the taqsh meant that there would be no figs when the time for figs came. For all its fair show of foliage, it was a fruitless and hopeless tree.

The whole incident was an acted parable. To Jesus the fig-tree, fair but barren, spoke of the city of Jerusalem, where he had found much religious observance, but no response to His message from God. The withering of the tree was thus an omen of the disaster which, as He foresaw and foretold, would shortly fall upon the city.[9]

It is dangerous, then, for the critic quickly to assume that an event which seems puzzling to twentieth-century readers cannot reasonably be viewed as religiously significant. It will not do for us to forget how distant we are from these events both temporally and culturally; closer investigation of the context in which they occurred may well prove embarrassing. Lest I be taken to be claiming more than I intend, let me hasten to add that I am not assuming this will prove the case. All I am saying is that the critic needs to be very careful in her use of this objection and realize that, in the absence of detailed knowledge of the situation in which the miracle took place, it cannot be strongly pressed.

Miracles and God's Perfection

A second objection that is sometimes raised is that miracles imply some imperfection in God. Thus Peter Annet, a deist writing prior to Hume, objects that

God has settled the laws of nature by His wisdom and power, and therefore cannot alter them consistent with His Perfections. This is a demonstrative proof of the impossibility of miracles *a priori*; and if the effects change, so must the cause; if the laws alter so must the law giver. This proves the same *a posteriori* ... [It] is to suppose His Will and Wisdom mutable; and that they are not the best laws of the most perfect Being ... If the course of nature is not the best ... and fittest that could be it is not the offspring of Perfect Wisdom nor was it settled by Divine Will. [10]

On this conception, miracles must be understood as implying a lack of foreknowledge; they are seen as a makeshift means to deal with some unforeseen obstacle to the Divine Will. A God who performs miracles, so the objection runs, must be conceived as analogous to a beginning painter who paints his way into a corner and then cannot get out except by undoing some of his previous work. As Annet adds:

If God ever determined ... to interpose ... by a different method than that of his standard laws; it must be either because he could not foresee the consequences, which is like blundering in the dark; or he foresaw it would be needful; and then it would be like a blunder in the design and contrivance; or he foreknew and determined his own works should not answer his own ends, without his mending work, which is worst of all. [11]

This objection cannot be sustained, however. Most theists maintain that God has endowed man with free will and consequently a capacity to influence history. They also maintain that God has certain purposes and wants to see these fulfilled. Given the apologist is prepared to defend these two beliefs, it does not seem implausible that God might not at times intervene in the usual course of events so as to fulfil certain of His purposes which might otherwise be thwarted. As F.R. Tennant observes, the objection that miracles imply an imperfect God is based on the rationistic prejudice of the deists.

[T]he [deistic] idea of God is that of ... [an] immutable an "perfect" Being, the idea of the world is that of the block universe ... and the idea of law is that of an absolutely settled order which it behooves God to leave well alone. If, on the contrary, ... the world ... [has] a derived or devolved activity permitted to it, as relatively independent of its self-limited Creator; and if any of God's creatures are in their lesser way also creators: then ... why should not God encounter obstacles within His own created world? Is it not inevitable that He will do so? The deists were so shocked at the attribution of anything like arbitrariness to the Deity that, in their zeal to rule it out, they also by implication removed all possibility of God's directivity, of adaptation of immutable purpose to emergent needs. In their haste to eliminate from the idea of God the very anthropic quality of caprice and changefulness, they ascribed to Him the equally anthropic qualities of indifference and impassive obstinacy. [12]

MIRACLES AND THE PYRRHONISTIC FALLACY

Shifting her attack from theoretical to more practical matters, the physicalist might attempt to argue there is no good evidence that miracles occur. She might claim that all purported miracles are most plausibly accounted for on the basis of alternative physicalist hypotheses and attempt to explain them in terms of ignorance about the workings of nature, love of wonder, a desire to deceive the reader, or some other non-supernatural cause.

At the very least, detailed consideration of this claim would involve a lengthy excursion into the subject of Christian evidences, an excursion beyond the scope of this book. Aside from the issues I have already discussed in my previous chapter on evidence, I will limit myself to making two very general points. The first is that the physicalist

must be careful not to commit the Pyrrhonistic error of supposing that, because some accounts of miracles can easily
be dismissed, all accounts of miracles can be dealt with
thus. As Lewis notes,

> no one really thinks that ... the Resurrection is exactly on the
> same level with some pious tittle-tattle about how Mother Egaree
> Louise miraculously found her second best thimble by the aid of
> St Anthony. The religious and the irreligious are really quite
> agreed on the point. The whoop of delight with which the sceptic
> would unearth the story of the thimble, and the "rosy pudency"
> with which the Christian would keep it in the background, both
> tell the same tale. Even those who think all stories of miracles
> absurd think some very much more absurd than others: even
> those who believe them all (if anyone does) think that some
> require a specially robust faith. [13]

One need only compare the reports of miracles found in the
canonical Gospels with those found in the Apocryphal
Gospels to realize the truth of Lewis's claim.

Second, it would be a mistake, although an understandable one, for the physicalist not to question the scepticism current among modern theologians concerning our
knowledge of the historical Jesus. All too often, they uncrit-
ically accept an inadequate methodology which, if consistently applied, could be used to discredit the historical
reliability of practically any document. To mention but one
example, there is a distressing tendency among many
engaged in New Testament criticism to seek alternative
interpretations of accounts that purport to be historical.
One frequently encounters the supposition that if there
exists any parallel to a Gospel incident in the Old Testament then we must assume the Gospel writer invented the
story. Why this should be assumed *a priori*, why even if Elijah multiplied food (1 Kings 17:7–16) Jesus might not have
performed a similar miracle, is never made explicit, but it is
on the basis of this assumption that the Gospel record of the

event is dismissed as unhistorical and regarded as an invention of the early Church.

The point I am making, of course, is that the physicalist cannot simply assume that the miracles recorded in the New Testament are pious legends invented by a credulous church. Neither the remarkable accuracy of the New Testament documents concerning historical, cultural, and geographical detail nor the early date at which these accounts came into existence lend themselves to this view. *Prima facie*, these documents constitute testimonial evidence that miracles have occurred. Given their reliability in other areas where their accuracy can be checked, the burden of proof is upon the physicalist if he wishes to dismiss their worth as evidence.

MIRACLES, THEISM, AND ALTERNATE WORLD-VIEWS

Earlier, I postponed the question of whether the concept of a miracle is a uniquely theistic one or whether it can be integrated into a non-theistic world-view. It is clear it can find no home in a physicalist metaphysic, but it would be a mistake to assume that physicalism is theism's only rival. A brief discussion of other non-theistic world-views and their possible accommodation of the concept is therefore in order.

We may begin by noting that the rivals to theism are not many. Excluding physicalism, plausible alternative world-views are limited to pantheism and panentheism. It might be objected that in saying this I am ignoring polytheism and animism. My view on this matter is that polytheism and animism are not viable contenders for a suitable world-view. Their conceptual development invariably involves either a slide into theism, with the lesser gods and spirits being considered creations of one God, or into pantheism, where the gods and spirits are considered to be but appearances or aspects of the more fundamental One.

Pantheism and Miracles

The term "pantheism" is derived from the Greek words for "all" and "God." In many respects this world-view is the polar opposite of physicalism. Both are monistic systems positing only one kind of reality, but, whereas the physicalist maintains that all that is is physical, the pantheist holds that all that is is divine. In other words, the pantheist insists there is no ontological distinction between God and the world.

Although pantheism has proved attractive to both Eastern and Western thinkers and has received many impressive formulations, it is clear it cannot accommodate the concept of miracle; and for essentially the same reason physicalism cannot: it is a monism and cannot admit the reality of two ontologically distinct levels of being. A miracle implies the overriding of nature by something other than nature, a transcendent agent. Physicalism must fail to accommodate the concept of miracle in that it cannot admit the existence of something other than nature by which nature could be overridden; pantheism must no less fail in that it cannot admit the existence of something other than God for God to override.

Lest I be misunderstood, I want to emphasize that the pantheist is quite at liberty to question the evidence the theist cites as justifying belief in miracles or to question whether such events are best described as miracles. My point is not that the theist has demonstrated the occurrence of miracles, but that if he can demonstrate the occurrence of events that are best interpreted as being miracles these events will count not only against the truth of physicalism, but also against the truth of pantheism.

Panentheism and Miracles

Panentheism is best thought of as an attempt to develop a *via media* between pantheism and traditional theism.

Unlike pantheism, panentheism maintains that God and nature are not identical, but unlike theism it denies that God is the efficient cause of nature. In theism there is thought to exist an asymmetrical relation between God and nature: nature, although ontologically distinct from God, is dependent for its being upon God, but God's existence is in no way dependent on the existence of nature. Panentheism rejects this idea. God and the world are conceived as interdependent; God being thought of as not the efficient, but the formal, cause of the world.

Inasmuch as it allows a distinction between God and the world, it might be thought that panentheism can readily accommodate the concept of miracle. Such a conclusion would be premature. The reason it would be premature is that, although it is clear that certain apparently powerful objections to belief in miracles can be met if we employ the theistic concept of creation *ex nihilo*, it is not clear that they can be met with the conceptual apparatus available to the panentheist. The concept of creation *ex nihilo* is simply not available to the panentheist; to employ it would be to violate his claim that God cannot be the efficient cause of the world or things in the world, only the formal cause. To the extent that miracles are linked with the concept of creation *ex nihilo*, the panentheist will find it impossible to accommodate the concept of miracle into his system.

Seeing this allows a more general point to be made. It is that it is impossible in principle for the panentheist to allow the possibility of miracles. The concept of creation *ex nihilo* is important precisely because miracles imply that Goc can act as an efficient cause in the world. If we did not make appeal to concept of creation *ex nihilo* in discussing the possibility of miracles then we would have to make appeal to some other notion which explains how God can act as an efficient cause in the world. The concept of a miracle, therefore, is bound to prove impossible to incorporate into panentheism.

MIRACLES AND CHRISTIANITY

So far, we have been discussing the possibility that miracles may justify a theistic world-view over rival world-views. Establishing this is a major part of the Christian apologist's task. Not all theists are Christians, however, so it can scarcely be the whole of it. An important question, therefore, is whether an appeal to miracles can take the apologist any further in his task of defending Christianity.

At first glance, the answer to this question must seem to be an unqualified no. Other religions besides Christianity claim miracles and it would be rash, without a careful examination of the evidence, to assume that miracles have not occurred in these religions. The apologist can scarcely conclude that, because he can appeal to some well-evidenced miracle, his is the true religion and then proceed to rule against accounts of miracles in rival religions. If there is good evidence that miracles have occurred in other religions the apologist cannot hold that Christianity is true merely on the grounds that it can point to some well-evidenced miracles.

Indeed, even if it proves the case that rival religions cannot point to well-evidenced miracles and Christianity can, this does not guarantee the truth of Christianity, although it may go a long ways towards persuading us that Christianity is more plausible than its rivals. Miracles are usually performed by, or mediated through, a human person. The fact that a person exhibits remarkable abilities neither entails that he knows nor, if he knows, that he is truthful about the source and meaning of his power.[14]

There can be no question, therefore, of using miracles straightforwardly to establish the truth-claims of Christianity. It would be wrong, however, to conclude from this that miracles can have no role in establishing Christianity as opposed to some rival religion. The significance of a miracle stems from the context in which it occurs. To the degree that it is an isolated marvel, it has little significance and consequently little apologetic value, beyond casting doubt on the adequacy of non-theistic world-views. To the degree, though, that it is part of a large and meaningful whole it is significant and consequently has a good deal of apologetic value. Although I do not want to pursue this point in detail, it is liable to seem vague and ambiguous in the absence of concrete examples. Consider two examples: Elijah's calling fire down from heaven (1 Kings 17:1–19:18) and the Resurrection of Jesus.

Seen merely as a spectacular and unique event, Elijah's calling down fire from heaven has little significance. It takes on greater significance, however, when we realize that the Jewish religion had all but disappeared because of the influence of the native religions of the area and Jezebel's persecution of those who worshipped Yahweh. Had Elijah failed, had he not succeeded in his contest with the four hundred and fifty prophets of Baal, Jezebel might well have been successful in eradicating Judaism.

Similarly, the significance of the Resurrection stems primarily from the context in which it occurred, not from its unusual and unique character. As Clark Pinnock notes:

In the historical apologetic based on the bodily resurrection of Jesus, it is important to observe the full *context* of the putative event. If the occurrence be wrenched from its setting like a severed toe and held up to view, of course the Christian significance of it cannot be registered ... If the apologist permits this to happen, all is lost. In fact no one ever comes to believe the sign of the resurrection of Jesus in this way, as an isolated and unrelated marvel. The resurrection event is part and parcel of a much longer narrative ... The historical apologist should not allow himself to be lured into the position of defending the resurrection as a naked event. Unbelief cannot be overcome by the production of a single fact, any fact ... Neither Flew nor Jesus' first century sceptics are going to be converted by the resurrection as a bare event, barring some rare Damascus road illumination. [15]

It is important, therefore, that the apologist provide us with some sort of perspective by which we can view such events and make sense of them. Thus, in discussing the Resurrection, it is important that the apologist mention that throughout the Gospels we find Jesus making references, sometimes veiled, to the significance of his coming death and resurrection. [16]

I suggest that the apologetic value of these miracles, and others like them, lies not in the fact that they are marvellous events which automatically demonstrate the truth of the system or doctrine with which they are associated. True, they are marvellous events which demand an explanation. Their real significance, however, lies in the fact that they are integral parts of a larger system. They function, to use one of the biblical words for miracles, as signs. Conjoined with a doctrine or claim which transcends reason in the sense that we could never arrive at it ourselves, but which is nevertheless consonant with reason, miracles provide grounds for accepting as revelatory those elements opaque to unaided reason. Thus, although the miracles of Christ, for example, do not in any strict sense prove His divinity, they do provide reason to take seriously his claims to be the Messiah. Assuming there is good evidence the miracles occurred, those who deny that Jesus is the Messiah must explain them in some other way. They must do this, it should be noted, in a way which accounts not only for the miracles, but also for Jesus' moral stature and claims of authority. [17] This, as the opponents of Jesus discovered when they attempted to attribute His miracles to Beelzebul, may prove no easy matter (Luke 11:14–22).

The critic is liable to protest that this gets us nowhere in trying to decide between rival religions. Surely any religion will see the miracles which occur within its tradition as validating its belief-system. If, then, it turns out there is good reason to believe that miracles have occurred in more than one religious tradition we are no closer to being able to choose one over the other. Miracles may help to establish the truth of theism, but they can be of no use in deciding between rival religions.

The critic has ignored two important facts, however. The first is that it is a mistake to think that the sole or even primary purpose of a miracle must be to ground the belief-system of the religious tradition in which it occurs. It seems quite possible that even if a person had a mistaken conception of Him or denied His existence altogether, God might perform a miracle in order to alleviate human misery.

What this suggests is that miracles may conceivably occur within religious traditions which cannot readily accommodate them into their belief-structures. Thus, for example, we read of miracles within the Buddhist tradition, even though the general thrust of Buddhism is to deny the existence of God and the reality of the physical world. Whether or not there is sufficient evidence to justify belief in these miracles is not the point. Rather, it is that, even if miracles have occurred within the Buddhist tradition, they do not serve as evidence of its truth. Indeed, inasmuch as they presuppose the truth of certain concepts which Buddhism denies, they serve as evidence against its truth.

The second fact that the critic ignores is that all miracles, not just the ones associated with a particular religious tradition, require explanation. Given this, it is at least possible that one religion will be able to account for the miracles associated with its rival, but not vice versa. Christians, for example, have no particular problems accepting the miracles associated with Judaism, but Jews can scarcely accept the Resurrection of Jesus. If, then, there is good evidence that the Resurrection occurred, this would count in establishing Christianity over Judaism.

This, of course, is not to suggest that all, or even most miracles, provide means of adjudicating between rival religions. Nor is it to suggest that there are no other ways of deciding the question. It is merely to assert that the critic goes too far in claiming that miracles can have no role in this task. How great a role they can actually have cannot be stated in advance of examining the particular miracles and religions in question. That, however, is a different issue and one properly the subject of another book. What is evident is that if we have good evidence that miracles occur we have good reason to reject non-theistic world-views and perhaps some grounds upon which to evaluate rival theistic religious traditions.

Notes

1 THE TASK OF DEFINITION

1 Flew, "Miracles," 346.
2 Holland, "The Miraculous," 43.
3 Ibid., 44.
4 David Hume commenting upon miracles wrote that "if a person claiming a divine authority should command a sick person to be well, a healthful man to fall down dead, the clouds to pour rain, the winds to blow – in short, should order many natural events, which immediately follow upon his command – these might justly be deemed miracles ... *if any suspicion remain that the event and command concurred by accident, there is no miracle ... "* (*An Inquiry Concerning Human Understanding,* 120; emphasis added).
5 For a discussion of some of the difficulties associated with the notion of miracles as coincidences see J.C.A Gaskin, "Miracles and the Religiously Significant Coincidence," and Ian Walker, "Miracles and Coincidences."
6 Hume, *An Inquiry Concerning Human Understanding,* 120.
7 Swinburne, *The Concept of Miracle,* 9.
8 Basinger and Basinger, *Philosophy and Miracle,* 22.
9 See, for example, G.C. Berkouwer, *The Providence of God,* 208. Also see Francis MacNutt, *Healing,* 77–95.
10 Ramm, *Protestant Christian Evidences,* 126.
11 My point is that in the case of some events, such as willed bodily actions, it is much more a matter of debate whether

they must be explained in terms of the action of agents who, to some degree, transcend nature. `

2 MIRACLES AND THE LAWS OF NATURE

1 Flew, *God and Philosophy*, 148–9.
2 Ibid., 150.
3 Odegard, "Miracles and Good Evidence," 37–46.
4 Swinburne, *The Concept of Miracle*, 27–8.
5 My point is that, even if we assume the laws of nature are absolute and not statistical, miracles need not be conceived as violating the laws of nature.
6 C.E.M. Joad put the distinction I am making particularly well when he wrote that, "science will never succeed in dispensing with the necessity for postulating a something which is regarded as that to which at any given moment its laws are applicable, and this something, from the very fact that it is its working and consequences which scientific law maps and predicts, must itself be other than the operations of law ... Science ... analyzes the world into a comparatively featureless and therefore unknown X, collocations, stuff, matter – the name we give to it is immaterial – and the laws which govern its behaviour" ("The World of Physics and of Plato," 162–3).
7 Dorothy Sayers, *The Man Born to Be King*, 311–12, has some interesting speculations along these lines.
8 John Collier ("Against Miracles," 352) has suggested that my account of miracles as involving the creation or annihilation of energy implies a violation of natural law, since the notion of an unmoved mover implies the falsity of Newton's Third Law of Motion, sometimes called the Law of Reaction. What Collier ignores is that this law refers to the relation between two physical objects. However, God is not a physical object and the relation between God and that which He creates or annihilates is not a physical relation. It makes no sense, therefore, to suggest that God's creation or annihilation of energy is inconsistent with Newton's Third Law. What is true is that any new physical objects God creates will both act upon and be acted upon by previously

existing physical objects. Lest Collier protest that I have made life easy for myself by only considering cases of creation, let me point out that the Third Law concerns the *relation* between two physical objects. If, because God has annihilated it, one of those objects no longer exists there can be no physical relation between it and the other object, and thus there can be no question of the Third Law being violated. Collier fails, therefore, to show that my account of miracles implies violation of the laws of nature.

3 DAVID HUME AND PRIOR PROBABILITY

1 Flew, *Hume's Philosophy of Belief*, 176.
2 Ibid., 185–6.
3 Hume, *An Inquiry Concerning Human Understanding*, 115.
4 R.M. Burns, *The Great Debate on Miracles*, 144.
5 Ibid., 146.
6 Hume, *An Inquiry Concerning Human Understanding*, 119.
7 Ibid., 120.
8 There are a number of these scattered throughout Part II of the essay. Besides the comment already mentioned, the most notable examples are Hume's remark concerning the well-attested Jansenist miracles: "And what have we to oppose to such a cloud of witnesses but the absolute impossibility or miraculous nature of the events which they relate? And this, surely, in the eyes of all reasonable people, will alone be regarded as a sufficient refutation" (*An Inquiry Concerning Human Understanding*, 128).
  See also his thinly veiled comment concerning the resurrection: "But suppose that all the historians who treat of England should agree that on the first of January, 1600, Queen Elizabeth died; that both before and after her death she was seen by her physicians and the whole court, as is usual with persons of her rank; that her successor was acknowledged and proclaimed by the Parliament; and that, after being interred for a month, she again appeared, resumed the throne, and governed England for three years – I must confess that I should be surprised at the concurrence of so many odd circumstances, but should not have the

least inclination to believe so miraculous an event. I should
not doubt of her pretended death and of those other public
circumstances that followed it; I should only assert it to
have been pretended, and that it neither was, nor possibly
could be, real. You would in vain object to me the difficulty and almost impossibility of deceiving the world in an
affair of such consequence; the wisdom (and integrity) and
solid judgment of that renowned Queen, with the little or
no advantage which she could reap from so poor an artifice
– all this might astonish me, but I would still reply that the
knavery and folly of men are such common phenomena
that I should rather believe the most extraordinary events
to arise from their concurrence than admit of so signal a
violation of the laws of nature" (Ibid., 134).

9 Ibid., 127.
10 See Burns, *The Great Debate on Miracles*, 153.
11 Flew, *Hume's Philosophy of Belief*, 205.
12 1 Kings 17:14–16; Luke 9:16–17.
13 C.D Broad, "Hume's Theory of the Credibility of Miracle,"
   86.
14 See, for example, Gary Colwell, "On Defining Away the
   Miraculous," 330.
15 Broad, "Hume's Theory of the Credibility of Miracle," 87.
16 Hume, *An Inquiry Concerning Human Understanding*, 119.
17 Broad, "Hume's Theory of the Credibility of Miracle," 87.
18 Hume, *An Inquiry Concerning Human Understanding*, 118.

4 FURTHER OBJECTIONS TO MIRACLES

1 Alastair McKinnon, "Miracle and Paradox," 308.
2 Ibid., 309.
3 Ibid.
4 Ibid.
5 Ibid.
6 Ibid., 310.
7 Ibid.
8 Basinger and Basinger, *Philosophy and Miracle*, 11, make
   the same point, although we have arrived at it independently. They write: "Natural laws – even those which are

considered universal – are conditional propositions. They
do not describe what will or will not occur, given *any set* of
preconditions. Natural laws tell us that, given a specific set
of natural conditions *and given that there are no other relevant forces present*, certain natural phenomena will or will
not always occur."

9 Patrick Nowell-Smith, "Miracles – The Philosophical
Approach," 395.

10 Ibid., 396.

11 Ibid.

12 Ibid., 399.

13 Ibid., 397.

14 See, for example, Richard Swinburne, *The Concept of
Miracle*, 53–4.

15 Ibid.

16 Ibid., 54.

17 George Chryssides, "Miracles and Agents," 322.

18 Ibid., 319.

19 Ibid., 322.

20 Ibid., 323.

21 Ibid.

22 Norman Geisler, *Miracles and Modern Thought*, 44.

23 Guy Robinson, "Miracles," 159.

24 I am aware that phrases like "moral and religious significance" tend to be somewhat vague. The point I am trying
to make in introducing this criterion is put very well by
Bernard Ramm, who writes: "It may be safely asserted that
a hypothesis does not receive fair treatment if viewed dis-
connected from its system, and further, that any hypothesis
proposed must make peace with the system that it is associated with – even to revolutionizing the system, e.g.
Copernicus and Einstein. It is therefore impossible to see
miracles in the Christian [religious] perspective if viewed
only as problems of science and history, i.e. to use only historical and scientific categories for interpretation. It is not
asked that miracles be accepted blindly simply because they
are associated with the Christian system; nor do we argue
in a circle asking one to view miracles from the Christian
position to see them as true when the Christian system is

the point at issue. No hypothesis in science is confirmed until tentatively accepted as true. The tentative acceptation does not prove the hypothesis but it is absolutely necessary to test the hypothesis" (*Protestant Christian Evidences*, 129).

25 N.L. Geisler, *Christian Apologetics*, 272.
26 David Basinger, "Miracles and Apologetics: A Response," 349.
27 See Margaret Boden, "Miracles and Scientific Explanation," 137–44, for a good discussion of this issue.
28 Grace M. Jantzen, "Hume on Miracles, History, and Apologetics," 324.
29 John Henry Newman, *Two Essays on Biblical and on Ecclesiastical Miracles*, 53–4.
30 Ibid.

5 PHYSICALISM AND THE CONSERVATION OF ENERGY

1 By physicalism I mean a species of philosophical monism according to which all that exists and is truly real is physical.
2 Carl G. Hempel, "Studies in the Logic of Confirmation," 32.
3 Mary Hesse, *The Structure of Scientific Inference*, 146.
4 Hempel, "Studies in the Logic of Confirmation," 32.
5 Ibid.
6 The critic may be tempted to object that I am using the term *confirmed* in an unusual way. Often, in philosophy of science, *confirmed* is taken simply to mean that the theory in question is consistent with the available empirical evidence. It is contrasted with the stronger term *justified* which is taken to mean that the theory in question is not only consistent with the available empirical evidence, but has logical and conceptual elements in its favour. My intention, in using the word *confirmed* in the way I have, has not been needlessly to obscure the issue, but to make an important point in non-technical language. I think my use of the word is close to our ordinary usage, but nothing hangs on this. If the critic prefers, the distinction I have

drawn between a theory being plausible and a theory being confirmed can be made in more technical language. The important point is not the language we use, but that we do distinguish between hypotheses which we merely entertain as possibly true, even though they are consistent with our available evidence, and hypotheses we think we have conclusive reasons for accepting. We do so on the basis of the amount of evidence available and the way it is linked to the hypothesis in question.

6 WORLD-VIEWS AND FALSIFICATION

1 Christine Overall, "Miracles as Evidence against the Existence of God," 347.
2 Ibid., 349.
3 Ibid., 350.
4 Ibid.
5 Ibid., 351.
6 Ibid.
7 Ibid.
8 Ibid.
9 Ibid.
10 Ibid.
11 David Basinger, "Miracles as Violations: Some Clarifications," 6.
12 Irving M. Copi, *Introduction to Logic*, 156–7.
13 Overall might be tempted to protest that I have been unduly harsh here. I do not think I have. Granted the idea that a miracle involves a violation of a law of nature is a time-honoured one, to attempt to define a miracle solely as a violation of a law of nature is to stray very far from how the term is actually used. At best, the idea that a miracle involves a violation of a law of nature expresses a necessary condition (I do not think it is even a necessry condition), not a sufficient condition. Similarly in the case of defining a miracle as an inexplicable event. Neither definition does justice to the richness of the term.
14 Overall, "Miracles as Evidence against the Existence of God," 351.

15 C.S. Lewis, *Miracles*, 73–4.

16 What I take to be Overall's objection is examined in chapter eight where I discuss Thomas Woolston's attack on the evidential value of miracles.

17 Ian Barbour says this concerning world-views: "We may use the term 'world-view' to designate ... a set of basic beliefs about the fundamental character of reality. World-views are realistic (they purport to reality) and inclusive (they include all of reality), but they represent only the features deemed significant as a framework for life-orientation. A metaphysical system, on the other hand, tries to represent exhaustively the most general characteristics of all events, and it arises from a more theoretical interest. But the distinction is never a sharp one, since world-views use metaphysical categories, and metaphysical systems reflect ultimate commitments which provide life-orientations" (*Issues in Science and Religion*, 261–2).

18 For example, a philosopher who adheres to a physicalist world-view, when called upon to give an account of the "religious sentiment," may consistently give a Freudian explanation or a Marxist explanation, or any one of a large number of explanations whose truth would be compatible with the truth of physicalism. What he is not a liberty to do is to accept an explanation whose truth would be incompatible with that truth. He cannot, for instance, offer as a possible explanation of "religious sentiment" the theory that God, a spiritual being, exists and instils this "religious sentiment" in certain of His creatures.

19 Imre Lakatos cautions: "There are no such things as crucial experiments, at least not if these are meant to be experiments which can instantly overthrow a research programme. In fact, when one research programme suffers defeat and is superseded by another one, we may – with long hindsight – call an experiment crucial if it turns out to have provided a spectacular corroborating instance for the victorious programme and a failure for the defeated one ... But scientists, of course, do not always judge heuristic situations correctly. A rash scientist may claim that his experiment defeated a programme, and parts of the scientific

community may even, rashly accept his claim. But if a scientist in the 'defeated' camp puts forward a few years later a scientific explanation of the allegedly 'crucial experiment' within (or consistent with) the allegedly defeated programme, the honorific title may be withdrawn and the 'crucial experiment' may turn from a defeat into a new victory for the programme" ("Falsification and the Methodology of Scientific Research Programmes," 173).

20 Although he is not talking explicitly of world-views, Lakatos (ibid., 155) suggests that one objective, as opposed to socio-psychological, reason to prefer one research program over another is that it explains the previous success of its rival and supersedes it by a further display of heuristic (explanatory) power. I take him to be making essentially the same point as I wish to make.

21 Clark Glymour, *Theory and Practice*, 150–2.

22 Ian Barbour, *Myths, Models and Paradigms*, 130.

23 John Thorp writes: "One thing which is clear is that there can be no such thing as agent causality – at least the radical kind of agent causality that the libertarian [and theist] wants – if one adheres to a mere regularity view of causation. Agent causality is, precisely, irregular. So that if there can be any content at all to the libertarian notion of agent causality it must be something other than regularity; it must be the idea of 'power' or one of its congeners" (*Free Will*, 101).

24 Paul R. Thagard, "The Best Explanation: Criteria for Theory Choice," 82.

25 Ibid., 89.

26 Ian Barbour, *Myths, Models and Paradigms*, 134.

27 Lakatos, "Falsification and the Methodology of Scientific Research," 174.

7 MIRACLES AND EVIDENCE

1 Gary Colwell, "On Defining Away the Miraculous," 332.

2 Swinburne, *The Concept of Miracle*, 33.

3 Ibid.

4 Ibid., 38.

5 Ibid., 39.
6 Flew, *God and Philosophy*, 145.
7 Flew, *Hume's Philosophy of Belief*, 187. See also *God and Philosophy*, 148–50, and "Miracles," 351.
8 Flew, *Hume's Philosophy of Belief*, 207–8.
9 Swinburne, *The Concept of Miracle*, 42–3.
10 Flew, *Hume's Philosophy of Belief*, 180.
11 Hume, *An Inquiry Concerning Human Understanding*, 121.
12 R.M. Burns, *The Great Debate on Miracles*, 237.
13 Hume, *An Inquiry Concerning Human Understanding*, 123.
14 Ibid.
15 Flew, *Hume's Philosophy of Belief*, 185–7.
16 Hume, *An Inquiry Concerning Human Understanding*, 122.
17 See, for example, George Mallone, *Those Controversial Gifts*; Charles E. Hummel, *Fire in the Fireplace: Contemporary Charismatic Renewal*: and Francis MacNutt, *Healing*.
18 George Campbell, *Dissertation on Miracles*, 108–11.
19 Hume, *An Inquiry Concerning Human Understanding*, 123.
20 See, for example, MacNutt *Healing*.
21 Hume, *An Inquiry Concerning Human Understanding*, 125.
22 Ibid., 133.

8 MIRACLES AND APOLOGETICS

1 R.M. Burns, *The Great Debate on Miracles*, 10.
2 Ibid., 12. Burns notes: "Not infrequently ... scholars seem to have approached the thought of this period with the assumption that they will find scepticism concerning miracles growing in direct proportion to the adoption of scientific attitudes, and at its keenest among those most influenced by modern science ... [H]owever ... this presupposition is not confirmed by the actual facts about the debate."

He continues: "In the first place, it must be realized that the stimulus behind the attacks on belief in miracles of this period was specifically theological: the sceptics had a theological axe to grind and cannot be regarded simply as advanced critical thinkers. Secondly, they were not the protagonists in the debate; it was their opponents, the advocates of belief in miracles, who began the debate by stressing the importance of miracles to a greater degree than ever before in the history of Christianity. The attack on miracles began as a defensive reaction to this development. Thirdly, those who emphasized the miraculous were not motivated by religious traditionalism; they were not conservatives, and their emphasis on miracles was only one of a series of novelties in their theological outlook. Fourthly, the believers in miracles, and not their opponents, may more plausibly be regarded as the advanced thinkers of their age, most in touch with the scientific spirit. The new theology which laid such stress on miracles was in fact very closely connected with the movement which had brought about the scientific revolution in England, so much so that we can even speak of the existence of one integrated religioscientific philosophical outlook, which was at the basis of the scientific achievements of such men as Boyle and Newton, but out of which also sprang, and in complete harmony with it, the new emphasis on miracles. In fact, to speak of a 'conflict' between science and religion at this juncture is quite inappropriate. Far from being in actual or potential conflict, scientific attitudes and religious belief can be shown to exist symbiotically in the thought of such leading intellects of the period as Boyle, Wilkins or Glanvill" (12–13).

3 Rudolph Bultmann, "New Testament and Mythology," 5.
4 Stephen J. Wykstra, "The Problem of Miracle in the Apologetic from History," 161.
5 Herbert Burhenn, "Attributing Miracles to Agents – Reply to George D. Chryssides," 489.
6 John Henry Newman, *Two Essays on Biblical and on Ecclesiastical Miracles*, 47.
7 Thomas Woolston, *A Third Discourse on the Miracles of Our Saviour*, 6–8.
8 Ibid., 11.
9 F.F. Bruce, *The New Testament Documents*, 73–4.
10 Peter Annet, *Supernaturals Examined*, 44.
11 Ibid., 46.

12 F.R. Tennant, *Miracle and Its Philosophical Presuppositions*, 90–1.
13 C.S. Lewis, *Miracles*, 111.
14 Wykstra, "The Problem of Miracle in the Apologetic from History," 157.
15 Clark Pinnock, "Fails to Grasp Ontological Basis for Problems," 158.
16 Many passages could be mentioned, but to name only a few: Matthew 21:33–45, Mark 2:18–19, Luke 9:18–22, John 12:23–33.
17 See, for example, John W. Wenham, *Christ and the Bible*, especially "The Authority of Jesus as a Teacher," 43–61.

Bibliography

Ahern, Dennis M. "Miracles and Physical Impossibility."
Canadian Journal of Philosophy 7 (1977): 71–9.

Annet, Peter. *Supernaturals Examined in Four Dissertations on
Three Treatises*. London: F. Page 1747.

Austin, William H. *The Relevance of Natural Science to Theology*. London: Macmillan 1976.

Barbour, Ian. *Issues in Science and Religion*. Englewood Cliffs,
New Jersey: Prentice-Hall 1966.

– *Myths, Models and Paradigms*. London: SCM Press 1974.

Basinger, David. "Miracles and Apologetics: A Response."
Christian Scholars Review 9 (1979–80): 348–53.

– "Christian Theism and the Concept of Miracle: Some Epistemological Perplexities." *Southern Journal of Philosophy* 18
(1980): 137–50.

– "Miracles as Violations: Some Clarification." *Southern Journal of Philosophy* 22 (1984): 1–7.

Basinger, David and Randall Basinger. "Science and the Concept of Miracle." *Journal of the American Scientific Affiliation* 30 (1978): 164–8.

– *Philosophy and Miracle*. Queenston, Ontario: The Edwin
Mellen Press 1986.

Berkouwer, G.C. *The Providence of God*. Grand Rapids, Michigan: Eerdmans 1974.

Blackman, Larry. "The Logical Impossibility of Miracles in
Hume." *International Journal for Philosophy of Religion* 10
(1979): 179–87.

Boden, Margaret. "Miracles and Scientific Explanation." *Ratio* 11 (1969): 137–44.

Borowitz, Sidney. "Conservation of Mass-Energy." *The Harper Encyclopedia of Science*. New York: Harper 1963. 276.

Broad, C.D. "Hume's Theory of the Credibility of Miracles." *Proceedings of the Aristotelian Society* 17 (1916–17): 77–94.

Brown, Colin. *Miracles and the Critical Mind*. Grand Rapids Michigan: Eerdmans 1984.

Bruce, F.F. *The New Testament Documents*. Revised 5th ed., Grand Rapids, Michigan: Eerdmans 1953; rpt. 1960.

Bultmann, Rudolph. "New Testament and Mythology." In *Kerygma and Myth*, ed. H.W. Bartsch, trans. Reginald H. Fuller. New York: Harper and Row 1961. I: 1–44.

Burhenn, Herbert. "Attributing Miracles to Agents – Reply to George D. Chryssides." *Religious Studies* 13 (1977): 485–9.

Burns, R.M. *The Great Debate on Miracles*. East Brunswick, New Jersey: Associated University Presses 1981.

Byrne, Peter. "Miracles and the Philosophy of Science." *Heythrop Journal* 19 (1978): 162–70.

Campbell, George. *Dissertation on Miracles*. Edinburgh 1762; third, enlarged, and corrected ed., 2 vols., Edinburgh 1797.

Chryssides, George. "Miracles and Agents." *Religious Studies* 11 (1975): 319–27.

Chrzan, Keith. "Vindicating the Principle of Relative Likelihood." *International Journal for Philosophy of Religion* 16 (1984): 13–18.

Collier, John. "Against Miracles." *Dialogue* 25 (1986): 349–52.

Colwell, Gary. "On Defining Away the Miraculous." *Philosophy* 57 (1982): 327–37.

– "Miracles and History." *Sophia* 22, no. 2 (1983): 9–14.

Conway, David A. "Miracles, Evidence, and Contrary Religions." *Sophia* 22, no. 3 (1983): 3–14.

Copi, Irving M. *Introduction to Logic*. 6th ed., New York: Macmillan 1982.

Diamond, Malcolm. "Miracles." *Religious Studies* 9 (1973): 307–24.

Dietl, Paul."On Miracles." *American Philosophical Quarterly* 5 (1968): 130–4.

Dubs, H.H. "Miracles – A Contemporary Attitude." *Hibbert Journal* 48: 159–62.

Eaton, Jeffrey C. "The Problem of Miracles and the Paradox of Double Agency." *Modern Theology* 1 (1985): 211–22.

Erlandson, Douglas K. "A New Look at Miracles." *Religious Studies* 13 (1977): 417–28.

Fethe, Charles B. "Miracles and Action Explanations." *Philosophy and Phenomenological Research* 36 (1976): 415–32.

Fitzgerald, Paul. "Miracles." *The Philosophical Forum*, 17 (1985): 48–64.

Flew, Antony. "Hume's Check." *Philosophical Quarterly* 9 (1959): 1–18.

– *Hume's Philosophy of Belief*. London: Routledge and Kegan Paul 1961.

– *God and Philosophy*. London: Hutchinson 1966.

– "Miracles." In *The Encyclopedia of Philosophy*, ed. Paul Edwards. New York: Macmillan 1967. 5: 346–53.

– "Parapsychology Revisited: Laws, Miracles and Repeatability." *Humanist* 36 (1976) 28–30.

Gaskin, J.C.A "Miracles and the Religiously Significant Coincidence." *Ratio* 17 (1975): 72–81.

– "Contrary Miracles Concluded." *Hume Studies* 1985 Supplement: 1–14.

Geisler, Norman L. *Christian Apologetics*. Grand Rapids, Michigan: Baker Books 1976.

– *Miracles and Modern Thought*. Grand Rapids, Michigan: Zondervan 1982.

Gill, John B. "Miracles with Method." *Sophia* 16, no. 3 (1977): 19–26.

Glymour, Clark. *Theory and Practice*. Princeton: Princeton University Press 1980.

Green, Michael, ed. *The Truth of God Incarnate*. Grand Rapids, Michigan: Eerdmans 1977.

Hambourger, Robert. "Belief in Miracles and Hume's Essay." *Nous* 14 (1980): 587–603.

Hanson, Anthony, ed. *Vindications*. London: SCM Press 1966.

Hempel, Carl G. "Studies in the Logic of Confirmation." In his *Aspects of Scientific Explanation and Other Essays in the Philosophy of Science*. New York: The Free Press 1965. 3–51.

Hesse, Mary, *The Structure of Scientific Inference*. London: Macmillan 1974.

– "Criteria of Truth in Science and Theology." In *Revolutions and Reconstructions in the Philosophy of Science*. Bloomington, Indiana: Indiana University Press, 1980. 235–55.

Hoffman, Joshua. "Comments on 'Miracles and the Laws of Nature.' " *Faith and Philosophy* 2 (October 1985): 347–52.

Holland, R.F. "The Miraculous." *American Philosophical Quarterly* 2 (1965): 43–51.

Hume, David. *On Human Nature and the Understanding*. Ed. Anthony Flew. New York: Collier 1975.

Hummel, Charles E. *Fire in the Fireplace: Contemporary Charismatic Renewal*. Downers Grove, Illinois: InterVarsity Press 1978.

Jantzen, Grace M. "Hume on Miracles, History, and Politics." *Christian Scholar's Review* 8 (1979): 318–25.

Joad C.E.M. "The World of Physics and of Plato." *The Hibbert Journal* 49 (1950–1): 159–70.

Kellenberger, J. "Facts, Brute Facts and Miracles." *Sophia* 7, no. 1 (1968): 19–21.

Kim, Jaegwon. "Explanation in Science." In *The Encyclopedia of Philosophy*, ed. Paul Edwards. New York: Macmillan 1967. 3: 159–63.

Lakatos, Imre. "Falsification and the Methodology of Scientific Research." In *Criticism and the Growth of Knowledge*, ed. Imre Lakatos and Alan Musgrave. London: Cambridge University Press 1970. 91–196.

Landrum, George. "What a Miracle Really Is." *Religious Studies* 12 (1976): 49–57.

Langford, Michael J. "The Problem of the Meaning of 'Miracle.' " *Religious Studies* 7 (1971): 43–52.

Langtry, Bruce. "Hume on Miracles and Contrary Religions." *Sophia* 14, no. 1 (1975): 29–34.

– "Miracles and Rival Systems of Religion." *Sophia* 24, no. 1 (1985): 21–31.

Lewis, C.S. *Miracles*. London: 1947; rpt. London: Fontana 1974.

Lias, John James. *Are Miracles Credible?* London: Hodder and Stoughton 1883.

Mallone, George. *Those Controversial Gifts*. Downers Grove, Illinois: InterVarsity Press 1983.

MacNutt, Francis. *Healing*. Notre Dame, Indiana: Ave Maria Press 1974.

Mavrodes, George I. "Miracles and the Laws of Nature." *Faith and Philosophy* 2 (October 1985): 333–46.

McKinnon, Alastair. " 'Miracle' and 'Paradox.' " *American Philosophical Quarterly* 4 (1967): 308–14.

Montgomery, John Warwick. "Science, Theology and the Miraculous." *Journal of the American Scientific Affiliation* 30 (1978): 145–53.

Moule, C.F.D., ed. *Miracles: Cambridge Studies in Their Philosophy and History*. London: A.R. Mowbray 1965.

Mozley, J.B. *Eight Lectures on Miracles*. 3rd ed., London: Longmans, Green 1898.

Newman, John Henry. *Two Essays on Biblical and on Ecclesiastical Miracles*. London: Longmans, Green 1890.

Nowell-Smith, Patrick. "Miracles – The Philosophical Approach." In *Philosophy of Religion: Selected Readings*, ed. William L. Rowe and William J. Wainwright. New York: Harcourt Brace Jovanovich 1973. 392–400.

Odegard, Douglas. "Miracles and Good Evidence." *Religious Studies* 18 (1982): 37–46.

Overall, Christine. "Miracles as Evidence against the Existence of God." *The Southern Journal of Philosophy* 23 (1985): 347–53.

Owen, David. "Hume *Versus* Price on Miracles and Prior Probabilities: Testimonies and the Bayesian Calculation." *The Philosophical Quarterly* 37 (1987): 187–202.

Pinnock, Clark. "Fails to Grasp Ontological Basis for Problem." *Journal of the American Scientific Affiliation* 30 (1978): 158–9.

Pratt, Vernon. "The Inexplicable and the Supernatural." *Philosophy* 43 (1968): 248–57.

Ramm, Bernard. *Protestant Christian Evidences*. 1953; rpt. Chicago: Moody Press 1976.

Robinson, Guy. "Miracles," *Ratio* 9 (1967): 155–66.

Sayers, Dorothy. *The Man Born to Be King*. New York: 1943; rpt. Grand Rapids, Michigan: Eerdmans 1976.

Smart, Ninian. *Philosophers and Religious Truth*. 2nd ed., London: SCM Press 1969.

Sobel, Jordan Howard. "On the Evidence of Testimony for

Miracles: A Bayesian Interpretation of David Hume's
Analysis." *The Philosophical Quarterly* 37 (1987): 166–86.

Sorenson, Roy A. "Hume's Scepticism concerning Reports of
Miracles." *Analysis* 43 (1983): 60.

Swinburne, Richard. *The Concept of Miracle*. New York:
Macmillan 1970.

Taylor, A.E. "David Hume and the Miraculous." In his *Philosophical Studies*. London: Macmillan 1934. 330–65.

Tennant, F.R. *Miracle and Its Philosophical Presuppositions*.
Cambridge: Cambridge University Press 1925.

Thagard, Paul R. "The Best Explanation: Criteria for Theory
Choice." *The Journal of Philosophy* 75 (1978): 76–92.

Thornton, J.C., "Miracles and God's Existence." *Philosophy* 59
(1984): 219–29.

Thorp, John. *Free Will: A Defence against Neurophysiological
Determinism*. London: Routledge & Kegan Paul 1980.

Wadia, P.S. "Miracles and Common Understanding." *Philosophical Quarterly* 26 (1976): 69–81.

Walker, Ian. "Miracles and Violations." *International Journal
For Philosophy Of Religion* 13 (1982): 103–8.

- "Miracles and Coincidences." *Sophia* 22, no. 3 (1983): 29–36.

Wallace, R.C. "Hume, Flew and the Miraculous." *Philosophical Quarterly* 20 (1970): 230–43.

Ward, Keith. "Miracles and Testimony." *Religious Studies* 21
(1985): 131–45.

Wei, Tan Tai. "Recent Discussions on Miracles." *Sophia* 11,
no. 3 (1972): 21–8.

- "Professor Langford's Meaning of 'Miracle.' " *Religious
Studies* 8 (1972): 251–5.

- "Mr Young on Miracles." *Religious Studies* 10 (1974): 333–7.

Wenham, John W. *Christ and the Bible*. Downer's Grove, Illinois: InterVarsity Press 1973.

Woolston, Thomas. *Six Discourses on the Miracles of Our
Saviour and Defences of His Discourses*. London: 1727–30;
rpt. New York: Garland Publishing 1979.

Wykstra, Stephen J. "The Problem of Miracle in the Apologetic
from History." *Journal of the American Scientific Affiliation*
30 (1978): 154–63.

Young, Robert. "Miracles and Epistemology." *Religious Studies*
8 (1972): 115–26.
– "Miracles and Physical Impossibility." *Sophia* 11, no. 3
(1972): 29–35.

Index

Names

Annet, P. 119–20, 141 nn10–11

Barbour, I. 86, 138 n17, 139 nn22, 26
Basinger, D. 54, 79, 136 n26, 137 n11
Basinger, D. and R. Basinger 131 n8, 134–5 n8
Berkouwer, G.C. 131 n9
Boden, M. 136 n27
Boyle, Sir Robert 140–1 n2
Broad, C.D. 37, 134 nn13, 15, 17
Brown, C. ix
Bruce, F.F. 118, 141 n9
Bultman, R. 112, 141 n3
Burhenn, H. 115, 141 n5
Burns, R.M. 33, 133 nn4, 7, 134 n10, 140 nn12, 1, 140–1 n2

Campbell, G. 106, 140 n18
Chryssides, G. 49, 50, 51, 135 nn17–21, 141 n5
Collier, J. 132–3 n8
Colwell, G. 134 n14, 139 n1
Copi, I.M. 137 n12

Flew, A. 4, 17, 31, 32, 33, 34, 36, 100, 101, 102, 104, 131 n1, 132 nn1–2, 133 nn1–2, 11, 140 nn6–8, 10, 15

Gaskin, J.C.A. 131 n5
Geisler, N.L. 54, 135 n22, 136 n25
Glanvill, J. 140–1 n2
Glymour, C. 139 n21

Hempel, C.G. 64, 136 nn2, 4–5
Hesse, M. 136 n4
Holland, R.F. 6, 7, 8, 55, 131 nn2, 3
Hume, D. 9, 10, 31, 32, 33, 34, 36, 37, 38, 39, 40, 41, 43, 62, 63, 103, 104, 106,

119, 131 nn4, 6, 133 nn3, 5,
6, 133–4 n8, 134 nn9, 16,
18, 140 nn13, 14, 19, 21, 22
Hummel, C. 140 n17

Jantzen, G. 54, 56, 136 n28
Joad, C.E.M. 132 n6

Lakatos, I. 91, 138–9 nn19,
20, 27
Lewis, C.S. 81, 122, 138 n15,
141 n13

McKinnon, A. 44, 45, 46, 131
n1, 134 nn1–7
MacNutt, F. 131 n9, 140
nn17, 30
Mallone, G. 140 n17

Newman, J.H. 58, 117, 136
nn29–30, 141 n6
Newton, Sir Isaac 140–1 n2
Nowell-Smith, P. 46, 47, 88,
135 nn9–13

Odegard, D. 18, 132 n3

Overall, C. 75, 76, 77, 78, 79,
80, 82, 115, 137 nn1–10,
13, 14, 138 n16

Pasteur, L. 70
Pinnock, C. 127, 142 n15

Ramm, B. 131 n10, 135–6
n24
Robinson, G. 30, 51, 52, 135
n23

Sayers, D. 132 n7
Swinburne, R. 10, 18, 48, 79,
95, 96, 97, 101, 131 n7, 132
n4, 135 nn14–16, 139
nn2–4, 140 nn5, 9
Tennant, F.R. 120, 142 n12
Thagard, P. 90, 139 nn24, 25
Thorp J. 139 n23

Walker, I. 131 n5
Wenham, J.W. 142 n17
Woolston, T. 117, 118, 141
nn7, 8
Wykstra, S. 112, 141 n4, 142
n14

Subjects

Agency 9, 13, 23–4, 25, 46,
48–51, 79, 88, 89, 90, 93
Analytic truths 84, 93
Angels 9
Animism 123
Anomaly 52–3
Apocryphal Gospels 122
Apologetics 94, 11–30

Apostles 104, 106

Beelzebul 128
Burden of proof 102

Causality 6, 8, 36, 48, 50,
88. *See also* Agency
Confirmation 66–8, 85–7

Coincidence 7–8, 49–50, 57
Consilience 90, 92
Converse consequence condition 63–6
Creation *ex nihilo* 25, 125. *See also* Mass/energy
Crucial experiment 83. *See also* Falsifiability
Cursing of the fig tree 116–19

Deep structural assumptions 66, 68–70
Definition 3, 5, 15, 21, 38, 80, 81
Deism 108, 119, 120, 121
Demythologization 111–12
Dogmatism 92, 104
Dysteleological surd 77

Epistemic dissonance 81
Evidence: conflict of x, 17–18, 32–41, 102, 107–8; principles of assessing 96–8; types of 95–6
Evil: cognitive 76–82, 115; moral 115–16
Explanation: deductive-nomological 19–20; distinguished for description 47; distinguished from prediction 43–4, 47–51. *See also* Agency
Explanatory hiatuses 89–90

Fallacy of division 94–5
False miracles 14
Falsifiability 58, 76, 83–92
First Law of Thermodynamics 21, 24, 30. *See*

also Principle of the Conservation of Energy
Flew's "balance-of-probabilities" argument 100–2
Foreknowledge 120

Galileo's laws 64–5

Healing 4, 27, 56, 78
Holism 84–8
Hume's *a posteriori* arguments 103–9
Hume's *a priori* argument 43, 105, 109
Hume's "balance-of-probabilities" argument 34–5; alternative approach to 40–2; Flew's interpretation of 31–4; relation to physicalism 62, 73; traditional interpretation of 31–4. *See also* Hume's *a priori* argument

Immaterial agents 88–90, 93
Induction 19, 36, 66
Initial conditions 19, 46. *See also* Material conditions
Interactionism 23–4

Jansenist miracles 104, 133–4 n8

Kepler's laws 64–5

Law of nature 15, 17, 61, 100, 101, 102; definition of 19–21; distinct from actual course of events 21–2,

44–6; distinct from an
observed regularity of
nature 19, 21–3, 44–6; distinct from "stuff" of
nature 20–1; Hume's con-
ception of 36; lower-level
laws 66, 68; relation to
miracles 14–30
Laws of motion 20–1, 132–3
n8
Lazarus, raising of 28

Mass/energy, creation or
annihilation of 20, 21, 24,
27–9, 61–73, 85–6, 87,
132–3 n8
Material conditions 20, 21,
23, 46
Memory 96–7
Metaphysical predilections 90
Metaphysical presuppositions
54, 58, 83
Mind-body problem 23–4, 89
Miracle: criteria for 10, 12,
29–30, 52–3, 114, 117;
definition of 3–15; rela-
tion to doctrine 11–12,
107–9, 127–30; relation to
laws of nature 17–29;
thought to be a pseudo-
concept 17, 44–6, 88;
violation concept of x,
14–18, 20–30, 44–6, 50–1,
77, 79, 101–2
Miracle-claims, corrigibility of
53–6, 114
Multiplication of loaves and
fishes 8, 9, 28, 37, 107,
116, 122

Naturalism 54, 55, 56, 57,
58–9
Nature 4, 5, 8, 9, 11, 13, 14,
17, 46, 53, 55, 81, 96
New Testament criticism 92
122–3
Newman's "balance-of-probabilities" argument 57–8
Newton's law of gravitation
64–5

Occam's Razor 71, 72, 88
Other selves 89

Panentheism 123–5
Pantheism 123–4
Physical traces 99–100
Physicalism 61–73, 75, 76,
85–6, 87, 117, 121
Plausibility 66–8. See also
Confirmation
Poltergeist activity 13
Polytheism 123
Prayer 4, 82
Principle of the Conservation
of Energy: relation to evi-
dence 26–7, 42, 61–73,
85–7; two forms distin-
guished 24–6. See also
Falsifiability; Physicalism
Probability 35, 58, 94–5,
100–2
Providential events 8

Religious significance 5, 7, 8,
10–12, 13, 14, 52–3, 57,
116–19, 135–6 n24
Repeatability requirement
50–1

Resurrection of Jesus 8, 28,
    29, 54, 116, 127, 128, 129

Science 38, 57, 68, 78
Simplicity 90, 92
Substitution instance 64

Testimony x, 32, 33, 34, 35,
    39, 40–2, 100, 102, 103, 105
Theism 25, 26, 27, 76, 77,
    85, 86, 87–91, 93, 111–15

Virgin birth 21–3, 27, 28,
    107,116

Walking on water 9, 28
Willed bodily actions 131–2
    n11
Working assumptions 54
World-view 48, 73, 75–92, 93,
    113, 126, 138 nn17–18, 139
    n20